What Every Businesswoman Needs to Know to Get Ahead

PEGGY VAN HULSTEYN

What Every Businesswoman Needs to Know to Get Ahead

DODD, MEAD & COMPANY · NEW YORK

David, with love

Excerpts from *Jane Trahey on Women and Power* by Jane Trahey, copyright ©
1977 are reprinted by permission of Jane Trahey; excerpts from *The Joy of Money*
by Paula Nelson, copyright © 1975 by Paula Nelson are reprinted by permission
of Stein & Day Publishers.

Copyright © 1982, 1984 by Peggy van Hulsteyn
Published by Dodd, Mead & Company, Inc.
79 Madison Avenue, New York, N.Y. 10016
Distributed in Canada by
McClelland and Stewart Limited, Toronto
Manufactured in the United States of America
Designed by Nancy Dale Muldoon
First Edition

Library of Congress Cataloging in Publication Data

Van Hulsteyn, Peggy.
    What every businesswoman needs to know to get ahead.

    Reprint. Originally published: Santa Fe, N.M. :
Bentley Press, 1982.
    Bibliography: p.
    Includes index.
    1. Women in business. 2. Women executives. I. Title.
HD6054.V36   1984   658.4′09′024042   84-10255
ISBN 0-396-08422-2 (pbk.)

Contents

Acknowledgments

I agree with the writer Tom Wolfe, who feels that "writing is like having arthritis. It hurts every day." With this thought in mind I am grateful to the following people who helped make the writing of this book a joy rather than a pain. Special thanks go to all the women who allowed me to interview them. They were, without exception, gracious with their time, enthusiasm, ideas, and sisterhood.

I am indebted to all the women who have attended my management seminars; they taught me as much as I hope I taught them.

I wish to thank my brother, Robert Guttman, for his sage advice and my parents, Jane and Gene Guttman, for their encouragement.

I want to acknowledge Gene Barnes, who is a fine example of women supporting women.

I appreciate the moral support my good friends George and Carol Price and John and Lois Sherman gave me.

Thanks to Judy Lawrence for all her savvy advice.

A special kudo to Nancy Bené for her friendship and proof-reading skills.

I also want to thank Cynthia Vartan, my editor, and Roslyn Targ, my agent. I am grateful to Kay E. Radtke, who was instrumental in getting this book into the right hands.

My deepest and most heartfelt gratitude goes to my husband, David, whose humor, encouragement, editing skills, and general loving care were as necessary in the writing of this book as my typewriter.

Introduction

As a writer, I fervently believe in the power of the written word. Accordingly, during my fourteen years in the business world, I searched continually for words of wisdom (or, for that matter, words of any kind) which would answer the myriad questions that concerned me as a woman in business. My quest was to no avail.

Nowhere could I locate the definitive book about women in business. Recently, however, there has been a reversal of the situation, and I have been somewhat encouraged by the spate of books devoted to this subject. I have eagerly read all that I could get my hands on. Many were excellent and most taught me something I didn't know; all were thought-provoking—even if the feeling some provoked in me was anger. None, however, was exactly the book I had in mind for answering the plethora of questions I have had about the problems confronting today's businesswoman.

Not being able to find precisely the book I envisioned, I did what any self-respecting writer would do. I decided to write it myself. During the course of this ambitious undertaking, four goals have evolved.

First, I intend the book to be just what it says it is—a handbook. It is a compilation of many important and useful books, as well as magazine and newspaper articles, pertinent to the contemporary working woman. In this capacity it is a reference guide that should save the reader time, which is a businesswoman's most precious commodity. This book, in other words, is for you busy women who are interested in a one-stop reading center where all the practical information on making your working life easier can be found under one cover.

My second objective is to present a new and refreshing view of women in business. I was distressed to note that many of the books I read said, basically, "If you want to succeed in business, you must play follow the leader and imitate all the games that men play."

I have tried to present alternatives to this thesis, because I strongly disagree with it. It's not that I think everything men do in business is wrong. Au contraire! They have been thriving in the corporate world for centuries and have obviously done many things brilliantly. However, businesswomen are not, nor should they want to be, clones of businessmen. As Dr. Estelle Ramey, a renowned specialist in endocrine research and an oft-quoted feminist, observes: "It's not that one sex is better or worse than another, but that we are different. These differences should be valued like jewels, because nothing is more valuable in problem solving than different perceptions. When you have a problem to solve, the one thing you don't want is for everybody to be looking down your tunnel because they are going to see the same mistake at the end. They will see one small light at the end of the tunnel, and it's not going to reflect on the truth as it would if you could open up all kinds of tunnels and get light pouring in from various places."

I am in complete agreement with this view. Furthermore, I also feel strongly that women can bring their own special talents, strengths, and sensitivities to the business world, thereby making it a more productive and humanistic environment for both men and women.

If I had been doubtful on this score, my skepticism was laid to rest when I conducted interviews with businesswomen throughout the country. It was one of the most heartening and positive experiences of my career. I wish you could have been along to experience the excitement and good will that I felt.

This special group of women offered proof that women are succeeding in all walks of professional life and that they are willing to help and advise other women on their way up. Those I interviewed are women at the top of the corporate ladder and, as such, are extremely powerful and busy. Yet all took time out from their hectic schedules to talk honestly and forthrightly to me and hence to you. They were deeply interested in the lot of all working women, and, because of their concern, we can all reap the benefits of this new solidarity.

I was delighted with the enthusiasm and support that they

showed toward this book. I was also pleased to find that all were secure enough about who they were to share some of their basic business secrets.

My third objective is to share with you the insights I gleaned from these interviews. In order to make these more meaningful, I should acquaint you with these women and tell you how I chose them. They fall into two groups.

The first group are the SUPERWOMEN, professionals and executives who are leaders in their fields. This group includes such notables as Sarah Caldwell (director of the Opera Company of Boston), Dr. Estelle Ramey (professor of physiology and biophysics at Georgetown University and named one of *Ladies Home Journal*'s "100 Most Important Women in America, 1983"), Cathleen Black (president of *USA Today*, former publisher of *New York* magazine and associate publisher of *Ms.* magazine), Jo Foxworth (head of her own New York advertising and communications agency and 1981 National Headliner, the highest honor given by Women in Communications), and Gene Barnes, as well-known public relations specialist and television writer/producer.

To balance things out, I have also included interviews with a second group, the REAL WOMEN, that is, women a lot like me and, perhaps, like you. In the course of writing this book, many of my colleagues complained that they were getting fed up with hearing only about the superstars; rather, they wanted to hear about women who seemed "real" and whose problems they shared.

These REAL WOMEN are mostly in middle management positions, many inching their way to the top. Some may ultimately rise to prestigious positions, others may not. In any event, the reason for including them is that they experience real and current problems and have to struggle in their efforts "to have it all." They precariously juggle careers and marriage or social life and sometimes find the going tough. Most, however, have worked out solutions, many of which could make your own life run a little more smoothly.

My fourth objective in writing this book is to present a synopsis of my own experiences as a corporate woman and as an owner of a business. *What Every Businesswoman Needs to Know to Get Ahead* is an attempt to answer the multitude of questions that I was asked by women who seemed to think I had all the answers.

But, to be candid, there are no absolute truths and answers. I

don't profess to have any Merlin-type magic formulas. I do, however, have some tested theories gleaned from being a pioneer in
virtually uncharted territory. Some of my business secrets were
gained from painful encounters, others from experiments that
turned into victories. I would like you to profit from my experience and to share the frustration, the excitement, and the enjoyment that I have felt.

In the course of my peripatetic career, I have worked in the
Midwest, the East, the Sun Belt, and the Southwest. I have observed the business world from both sides of the desk—as the
employed and the employer. I have worked as a magazine editor,
a newspaper editor, and the public relations director of a major
movie company.

I have experienced most aspects of the advertising business,
from writing copy for a small country-and-western radio station
to serving as the copy chief for one of the largest advertising
agencies in the country. Ultimately, this path lead me to open
my own advertising agency, which taught me the pain and the
pride of being a "boss lady."

During the course of my eclectic career, I have been told I
should be at home taking care of my babies, informed that "this
is no job for a woman," and asked to make the coffee. For more
than a decade, I have juggled the problems of managing home,
marriage, and two children.

Often I have found the businesswoman's path a lonely one.
This book is my attempt to assuage some of the solitude that you
might feel on your executive voyage. It is especially dedicated to
the contemporary businesswoman who finds herself in new territory without any up-to-date road maps.

"What's in It for Me?"

As they say in my field, the advertising business, "What's in it
for me?" "Why," you ask as you are leafing through this intro-
duction at your favorite bookstore, "should I ultimately read your
book?" Glad you asked! This book has one other aim besides the
aforementioned ones (which should have already convinced you,
but you obviously are a tough customer and books are expensive
today). It will give you practical information that can be immediately incorporated into your life. *What Every Businesswoman
Needs to Know to Get Ahead* will make your job and your life

easier by giving you helpful hints on the following questions that you may have been asking yourself.

◇ Do you know how to handle power games that take place in your office or are you suffering from power failure?

◇ Can you gracefully turn down your boss's sexual advances without turning off your chances for a promotion?

◇ Do you organize your time efficiently or is it time you got organized?

◇ Can you fire someone firmly yet graciously or are you playing "fire escape" by avoiding this unpleasant task?

◇ Can you survive being fired? Unfortunately none of us is "fire-proof."

◇ Have you had your consciousness raised (i.e., are you conscious of the best way to ask for raises)?

◇ Do you and your husband manage the household chores together now that you both need a wife?

◇ Are you successfully handling the juggling act called "being a working mother" or are you losing your delicate balance?

These are just some of the questions answered in this survival manual that will save you time and money and in the process perhaps even make your life easier and more enjoyable. But enough of this ruminating. The time has come to tell you *What Every Businesswoman Needs to Know to Get Ahead.*

1
Fire Drill

HIRING, FIRING, AND OTHER BURNING ISSUES

"I can't type. I can't file. I can't even answer the phone."
Elizabeth Ray

Maybe you consider yourself the brightest young executive to hit the business field since Mary Wells Lawrence came to town. Perhaps you are a brilliant luminary, and maybe we will indeed be seeing your name in bright lights on the front pages of *The Wall Street Journal* before long.

However, before you purchase your own Greek island or invest in a seat on the New York Stock Exchange, there are some things you should know that will help make your meteoric rise even faster. The crux of the issue concerns your staff. Do they make you look even better than you are, or are they holding you back? If you hire only the best and the brightest, then perhaps you might consider putting a down payment on that island (and, while you're at it, even learn a little Greek folk dancing). If your team functions with all the grace and efficiency of the Keystone Cops, however, your future purchasing clout might not even buy you one square foot of Florida swampland.

HOW NOT TO SUFFER "STAFF INFECTION"—THE IMPORTANCE OF A GOOD STAFF

Napoleon, legend has it, surrounded himself with only brilliant ministers who would make him look good. He was also allegedly a "big enough man" to realize he should hire the best person for the job even if it were someone he personally hated. Richard K. Irish, author of *Go Hire Yourself an Employer*, feels

1

that too many executives meet their Waterloo because they don't hire the right people: "The mark of a first-rate executive is the quality of his staff. If they are all, in certain respects, smarter than the boss, it's a mark of genius. Strong people surround themselves with highly competent and disparate staff. First-rate people hire first-rate people. Second-rate people hire third-rate people."

Part of the trick of keeping a top-notch staff is knowing when and how to fire someone who doesn't reflect well on you. Corporate heads will be watching your hiring and firing ability, and you could even be replaced yourself if you don't make expedient decisions! As Irish puts it, "The best test of a manager is how he fires people."[1]

So how about it? What does your staff say about you? Did you hire your best friend Andrea as your assistant because she couldn't get a job anyplace else and you felt sorry for her? Or do you know the effective way to hire people? Do you know the proper interview techniques, or do you just hire the first person who stumbles into your office?

Do you check potential employees' references or are you a trusting type? (Say! Wasn't that you I saw buying the Brooklyn Bridge recently?) Do you have in mind the qualities you want in an employee or do you just blithely hope that someone will fit in?

Do you know the kindest way to fire someone? Most executives look forward to firing someone with the same enthusiasm they would for getting trapped in an elevator with an overbearing insurance agent. However, it must be done occasionally, so it's time to increase your Firing Skills.

Then there's the nasty problem of what to do if it is you who is being fired. Yes, even you! Most executives worth their briefcase will get fired at least once during their careers. Do you have a plan of action if this dastardly thing should happen to you? Do you need tips on how to survive? Can you recognize the telltale signs that a firing is approaching, or will you feel as naive as a Thanksgiving turkey when the ax falls? Do you know how to benefit from getting fired? Believe it or not, there are times when it can be a positive learning experience!

All of these hiring and firing techniques can enhance your power as an executive. So, since we want you to blaze trails of glory rather than watch your career go up in smoke, we'd better get on with the FIRE DRILL.

SPECIAL PROBLEMS FOR THE WOMAN EXECUTIVE

Hiring and firing can be especially tricky for a woman executive. Since you are still a comparatively new kid on the block, people will be paying close attention to everything you do. Many will be waiting for you to fall on your corporate face. The way you hire and fire is essentially a window on your world and everyone can look in. So, make certain you give Peeping Toms and Tomasitas something to look up to.

The Art of Hiring

Hiring is sometimes like betting on horses or throwing dice; it's a gamble. As Amy Greene, president of Beauty Checkers, a company that teaches women how to apply makeup, puts it, "Sometimes all you can do is hire and hope." To improve your odds slightly, here are some tips to put you on the right track.

Hire the best now so you don't have to fire the worst later. Hiring may be the most important thing you will ever do as an executive, so do it well. Always keep the thought in mind that it's much simpler to take great pains over whom you hire now than to suffer the excruciating pain of firing someone later.

The interview ritual. The interview is the single most important step in hiring the right people. Therefore, you should give it your undivided attention. Hold your phone calls, don't have people barging in, and allow yourself to be interrupted only for emergencies. Give the applicant a chance to shine (or bomb), but whatever you do, don't use the interview as an opportunity to show how busy and important you are.

"Better living through chemistry." A man sits in your office with a résumé that would knock the socks off the Queen Mother herself. However, despite his impeccable credentials, there's something about him that you don't like. You have no feeling of rapport, no human chemistry. Should you hire him? Probably not. Sally Richardson, subsidiary rights director for St. Martin's Press, advises: "The most important thing in hiring is to get somebody you like and that you can talk to."

I agree with Richardson, but I must amend her thought slightly. Remember that Napoleon didn't always love his ministers. Sometimes an exception is necessary: I think you can work successfully with someone that you don't like personally as long as you respect him or her. For instance, Charles, my business associate, and I used to fight like William Buckley and Gore Vidal. Although we liked each other, we didn't always see eye-to-eye on personal issues. Nevertheless, as an artist-writer team, we were terrific. Never have I respected anyone's artistic and advertising ability more than Charles'. As a creative team, we were as smooth as peanut butter and jelly. You don't always have to like someone in order to work well together, but you *must* respect him. Keep in mind that Gilbert and Sullivan could hardly tolerate one another socially, but their creative output is music to our ears.

Sometimes a little friction (like the sand in an oyster that produces a pearl) can result in something beautiful in a working relationship.   Charles and I were a prime example of two irritants producing pearl-like advertising. Keep in mind that often you need some new blood which, in turn, may require someone who doesn't think exactly as you do. Therefore, when making a hiring decision, heed Jo Foxworth, who says in *Boss Lady*, "Ask yourself, 'Do we think alike and if we don't, will the differences be destructive or will they create healthy friction?' "[2]

Obviously you don't want the Capulets and Montagues in the same office.   How will the new person you are hiring get along with your existing staff? Bear in mind, you want to build a team, not set up an armed camp! As Debby Miller, West Coast representative for Political Profiles, a political information firm, puts it, "One of my biggest concerns in hiring is how well the person is going to fit in. Our office is rather small; therefore, compatible personalities are essential. The efficiency of the office goes up considerably when there is good rapport between the people."

You wouldn't want to hire a smoker as the receptionist for the American Lung Association.   How appropriate is an applicant for the job? Use some common sense. As Amy Greene advises: "If a person interviewing for a position as the floor manager comes for an interview in four-inch heels, she obviously isn't going to work out." After all, a person who has to stand on her feet all day has to dress comfortably and appropriately for the role.

Remind yourself that your office isn't supposed to resemble a ward at Bellevue or a branch of the Salvation Army. Don't hire people with personal problems. Refer them to a good therapist and send them packing! I once made the mistake of hiring a woman who at first seemed like the poster girl for Mental Health. Little by little, however, her picture came to more closely resemble the portrait of Dorian Gray. It seems that her father was an alcoholic, her brother a schizophrenic, her mother an aging prostitute, and her fiancé played around a little—with young boys, no less. And these were just the good things.

Although Ellen (not her real name) was a crackerjack secretary, there were days she had trouble getting to her typewriter. She was either crying on my shoulder or pouring out her troubles to one of my partners. Furthermore, her absentee record would have made Johnny Carson look good. Naturally she eventually got her walking papers, but not before I vowed never again to play Ann Landers to an employee.

Don't give people false expectations about a job. If you want a secretary to remain a secretary, don't promise to turn her into a fairy princess at the stroke of midnight. Be honest with applicants. If the job is merely a secretarial one that will probably lead no further, make this fact crystal clear.

I once had a secretary who said she would be quite content with the job of typing and taking dictation. At first, Lauri was a gem. Little by little, however, I noticed she got a bit huffy when asked to perform a secretarial duty. She purportedly wanted "more responsibility." What she really wanted, as it turned out, was *my job*. Since I was perfectly happy with that job, however, I suggested she look for employment elsewhere.

The moral of the story is that Lauri was an ambitious woman who wanted to use a secretarial position to move on to bigger and better things. I admired her ambition; I wished her luck elsewhere. However, I learned to tell future applicants (until I was blue in the face) that if they wanted to be chairperson of the board, they were looking in the wrong place. I continually reiterated the same old repetitious redundancy, "This is a secretarial job, nothing more, nothing less. If you won't be happy with this type of job, go someplace else."

On the other hand, if the job will lead to loftier positions, make that very clear to the person being interviewed. Ask the interviewee what her long-range goals are, how ambitious she is, if she is interested in a job where there will be opportunities to learn, and if she is willing to take on responsibility. An ambitious applicant, by the way, will ask you questions about all these areas and make it obvious that she is interested in climbing the corporate ladder at marathon speed.

Ask the person, "How would you feel about working for a woman?" Many men and women have definite prejudices about working for a woman. Find this out before you hire someone. You don't need a person who is antagonistic toward you or your staff before the first day at work.

Jo Foxworth tells the following story that graphically illustrates some people's dislike of working for women: "The female reluctance to accept a Boss Lady rather than a boss was first brought home to me by a bright, attractive young woman who applied for a job as my assistant. We hit it off wonderfully. The work was exactly what she was looking for, the salary was right, and she had every qualification I had hoped to find. As I was at the brink of hiring her, she suddenly asked, 'By the way, shouldn't I meet the man I'll be reporting to?'

"I laughed merrily and said, 'I'm the guy!' expecting this news to be greeted with riotous applause. . . . Haltingly, painfully, she said, 'Well-l-l, gee now . . . I don't know. I'm sure you're a perfectly nice person and all that, but I just think I'd like it better if I worked for a man.' "[3]

Should you start your own good-old-girls network? As an avid feminist, I lean in favor of hiring other women. If I had a man and woman with exactly the same credentials and whom I liked equally well, I would probably give the woman the job. I would never, however, pick a woman merely because she was a woman. If she were decidedly unqualified or if I had no rapport with her, I would pick the man. However, I feel that since women are still discriminated against in the business world, perhaps this injustice can be partially offset if women in power do everything possible to give other women a chance to succeed. Remember that no woman is an island; we're all in this together.

In choosing your staff, then, let common sense prevail. You obviously don't want to alienate the entire company by hiring only women. As Jo Foxworth points out: "Base your personnel decisions on ability rather than sex. Gender is an accident, not a credential or a disqualification."[4]

FAMILIARITY BREEDS CONFIDENCE

To make certain you know a potential employee really well, have several interviews with her. First impressions are often deceiving. Try to observe the person in several different settings. You might, for example, hold some interviews away from your office to see if you get a different impression over lunch or cocktails. This is a person you will be with at least eight hours a day, five days a week, not just a blind date. Therefore, get to know her very well.

"The closest to perfection a person ever comes is when he fills out a job application form."
Stanley J. Randall

Some people think that checking references is a carry-over from the Dark Ages and consequently they often don't do it. Several shocking articles, however, have been published recently that describe how job applicants fabricate dynamic résumés composed of outrageous lies. You should realize, in other words, that an interviewee who claims he graduated summa cum laude from Harvard and spent a year as a Rhodes Scholar might actually have flunked out of Parsons Junior College.

Now this type of chutzpah might be just what you're looking for if you're hiring a wild advertising art director or a super purchasing agent who is glib enough to buy Manhattans from the Indians. However, if your business is a bit more straightforward or is one based on academic achievements, credentials count a great deal; you had better check those references.

As a further safeguard, hire someone "on trial" for three months. See how you like each other.

I'VE OFTEN MET A MAN I DIDN'T LIKE—QUALITIES TO LOOK FOR IN HIRING

There is no such thing as a completely objective interview. Even though I am certain you are the quintessence of fairness, maybe you have, let's say, an irrational hatred of tortoise-shell glasses (no doubt some Freudian reaction to too many childhood readings of "The Tortoise and the Hare.") Therefore, when a perfectly qualified person innocently comes through the portals of your office bedecked with tortoise-shell glasses, he has a strike

against him without ever knowing the reason why. A type of op-
tical disillusion, one might say.

Richard K. Irish discusses the subject of bias: "The best employers judge long and hard before they choose each employee.
At the same time, all judgment reflects prejudice. No one es-
capes." True to his word, he reveals that "No man wearing a
diamond ring ever found employment through me."[5]

NOBODY'S PERFECT BUT ME AND THEE, AND METHINKS THERE'S SOMETHING A LITTLE ODD ABOUT THEE

The following are qualities that I find admirable in people whom
I am considering hiring.

A sense of humor.   I can sometimes forgive other bad qualities if a person has a sparkling wit.

Stress for success.   A job candidate doesn't necessarily have
to be a Hemingway hero, but he should follow the Hemingway
code of "grace under pressure." Ask the applicant some tough
questions and see if he remains cool under fire.

Wishy-washy people should all be washed out to sea.   I like
employees who can make quick decisions and who are secure
enough to stand behind them.

It's some of their business.   If someone hasn't taken the time
and effort to research my business thoroughly, I figure I have no
business hiring her.

Someone who is considerate of my time.   "Better late than
never" may be an adage applicable to some situations, but it doesn't
describe someone I want working for me. A person who arrives
promptly for an interview and knows when it is time to make his
exit is someone I will watch carefully and consider hiring.

When running my ad agency, I experienced a stream of people
who walked in off the streets to "talk to me about a job." Many
of these presumptuous types had the audacity to be offended when
I politely told them that I didn't have time to see people without
appointments. Drop-ins are quickly dropped from my hiring list.

Someone who is polite enough to write a thank-you note.   I
happen to be a stickler for good manners, and a well-written thank-
you note after an interview pleases me no end. It shows consideration and good business etiquette. I know that some executives
couldn't care less about this nicety and consider it just one more

detail to clutter up their desks. However, I guess I am just a throwback to a more civilized era when such common courtesy was commonplace.

People who can speak the King's English. I find inarticulate types a royal pain in the neck. Eloquence and a lively repartee speak well for any job applicant.

Someone who is cheerful and optimistic without being as saccharine as Pollyanna. This person would probably be a team player and would fit in well with the rest of the staff. Moody, eccentric types might liven up a cocktail party, but they are generally difficult to work with on a day-to-day basis.

A good confidence man. Someone who acts self-assured makes me feel confident. Don't forget that there's a big difference between confidence and arrogance. A confident type can ask for money comfortably and can calmly answer, "I don't know," to a question rather than inventing some far-fetched reply.

Game players should be in Las Vegas, not in my office. I like straightforward people who don't play games. Honesty and sincerity are traits right out of the Girl Scout's handbook, which is okay with me, since I happen to be a big fan of Juliette Low. (As you are no doubt aware, I was quite a terrific Girl Scout in my day.) By the same token, watch out for phonies. You can generally spot one on the first interview.

Enthusiasm. Wow! Do I ever like enthusiastic people who seem genuinely eager to learn.

Someone who is eminently qualified. Obviously I want someone who is tops in her field. Unless I am looking for an intern or a trainee, I am interested in someone who will become profitable to the company in a short period of time. I am also impressed with someone who knows exactly what he wants to do for me rather than a person who says something vague to the effect of, "Well, advertising looks like fun; besides, what else could I do with an English Lit major?"

Is she dressed for the part? Obviously an attractive, well-groomed appearance is vital for almost any job. As discussed in the chapter entitled *Judging a Book by Its Cover*, good body language, an appropriate handshake, and eye contact are all part of successful physical presentation.

PREFERENTIAL TREATMENT

The above are traits important to me, but, more importantly, most of them are generally considered signs of a good overall employee. There may be cases where your preferences may be different. Make certain, however, that you know what they are. Don't interview fifty people and *then* ask yourself what type of person you are looking for. The proper time to make your own check-off list of qualities that are important to you is before the first interviewee steps through your door.

CONSIDER THE MORAL RESPONSIBILITY YOU HAVE TOWARD YOUR JOB APPLICANTS

Remember that it hasn't been long since you sat on the other side of that desk, wondering if you were going to get the job. So, don't let your employer power give you amnesia. You know how nervous and anxious you were to find out if you got the job. People haven't changed at all in this respect since the days of yesteryear when you were out pounding the pavements like them. Debby Miller tells how she deals with people she is considering hiring: "It's absolutely essential to be fair to them. During the interview, I would tell them when I was going to get an answer to them, one way or another. When I made my decision, I made certain that I had called everyone whom I had interviewed to let them know that the job had been filled, so they didn't keep wondering. After all, you are playing around with people's lives!"

FIRE WORKS

Unless you are the Marquis de Sade reincarnate, you will not eagerly anticipate the firing of any employee. Any sensitive person would look forward to firing with about as much enthusiasm as she would to attending a convention of halitosis sufferers. Firing can be an odious experience.

Firing people, however, is a part—albeit an unpleasant one—of the package of being an executive: "With privilege goes responsibility."

Some women find firing an especially disturbing task because their upbringing taught them to want everyone to like them. If you were raised never to hurt anyone's feelings, then you may feel like a Simon Legree when you have to discharge someone. Firing triggers the "sin of perfection" mechanism in some women. In "Fear of Firing" (*Savvy,* September 1983), it is reported that "Some executives say they need a stiff drink or a Valium before or after doing the deed; others are so shaken they may take a day off. Donna E. Shalala, president of Hunter College of the City of New York, cried herself to sleep the night after she first fired an underling. 'The employee was gracious—indeed, took it very well,' she recalls. 'I was a mess.' "

Women will quickly get over their "fear of firing" when they realize that the eyes of the corporate world are on them. How a woman handles firing strongly influences the way in which upper management sizes up her executive potential. If she crumbles under the stress of the firing line, she may be the next one to be fired.

Richard K. Irish puts it this way: "The lady who wields the ax will be called a 'bitch.' But . . . it is far better to be called names by those you show the door than to suffer the consequences of being a 'nice woman who can't make decisions.' "[6]

Improving Your Firing Skills

Well, the inevitable will arrive, and you will eventually have to fire your first employee. You haven't been able to sleep for two nights, your stomach feels like Mount Vesuvius, and you're chain-smoking again. What should you do? Tackle the problem at hand, the sooner the better. To make this onerous job somewhat easier, follow these fire-proof suggestions:

Give the person the benefit of the doubt. If the employee in question isn't measuring up to your expectations, let him know. It's only fair to tell him what you don't like about his work and give him a full chance to improve. Maybe you've never made it clear exactly what you expect.

Next, set a time period in which you expect the changes to take place. Don't be cruel, but state explicitly that if a transformation hasn't taken place in a month, you will have no choice but to fire him.

If this confrontation fails to produce satisfactory results, I'm afraid it's time to become the head of the Firing Squad.

IF THERE IS NO FIRE ESCAPE

1. Be as kind as possible.   Begin by offering whatever warm remarks you can conjure up about any real contribution the person has made to the corporation. Don't pull them out of a hat; try to be sincere.

Robert Townsend in *Up The Organization* kindly suggests that you "don't be needlessly cruel in firing someone. Figure out a reason that is true but enables him to preserve his ego. . . . If you don't feel compelled to destroy his self-regard, he can move on quickly without scars."[7]

2. Don't prolong the interview.   Spending several hours telling someone that he's fired constitutes cruel and unusual punishment. Get to the point and let the person get out of your office.

3. Keep it impersonal.   You're trying to keep a person's dignity intact. Don't say, "You're the biggest jerk we've ever had at The Barnstorming Buggywhip Corporation. Besides that, Joe tells me that you never wear socks that match." Instead, use only hard facts and first-hand data to justify the firing.

4. Don't say, "You'll be better off."   If there's one thing an axed person doesn't want to hear, it is that this firing is an act of kindness "for your own good." Save your humanitarian gestures for a Sunday school class you are teaching or for speeches, should you decide to run for political office.

5. Don't allow the firing to turn into "The Great Debate."   Firing time is not the occasion for a Lincoln–Douglas-type debate. Make it clear that the action is firm and final.

Sally Richardson suggests saying something to the effect, "Let's not spend a lot of time trying to analyze why it isn't working."

6. Think of a firing as an intellectual rather than an emotional problem.   Even though firing someone is unpleasant, try to think of it as just part of your job and not as something personal.

STOP BEING YOUR OWN JEWISH MOTHER

Nothing plays on the old guilt more than the act of firing someone. Richard K. Irish, however, suggests that you will feel less guilt-ridden once you realize that by not firing the ineffectuals, you risk demoralizing the effective people. "In school, we *should* fail students. Not doing so harms those who do excellent work."

There is something far worse than firing people, Irish contends. "We are passed over for promotion, blocked from the next logical step in an organization, shelved . . . not the electric chair, but solitary confinement. . . . And as for 'human feeling,' what is more unfeeling than to let someone 'turn . . . and twist slowly in the wind'?"[8]

TRY TO HELP THE FIREE FIND A NEW JOB

Outplacement, the diplomatic term for helping a fired person find a new job, has become almost standard operating procedure for most companies. It's not that the former firm of Large and Heartless has changed its name to Small and Compassionate; there are very practical reasons for using outplacement. As the article "When The Ax Falls" (*Working Woman,* December 1983) states: "One is public relations, both external and internal. The community won't regard the company as a monster and an ex-employee won't badmouth the company or industry, and employees who remain will see that their former associates are being treated well. Another is avoiding lawsuits; a former employee who is focusing on getting that next job is less likely to think about suing her employer for firing her in the first place.

"Finally, there is a financial advantage. Companies hoping to trim their payrolls find that managers are less reluctant to terminate employees if they feel those people will be helped in finding new jobs. And with the aid of outplacement, ex-employees are likely to find those jobs more quickly than they might on their own. For companies that pay severance until a former worker locates a new job, outplacement may mean substantial corporate savings."

Nobody's Fire-proof—It Could Even Happen To You!

Being fired has to be one of life's unhappier experiences. I'd rather face a gang of motorcycle outlaws!

But if you do someday happen to get canned, don't just stew over your fate. Consider some of the following suggestions on how to handle it:

1. Keep your dignity. Accept the news of your firing calmly and unemotionally. Staying under control may be the most diffi-

cult thing you will ever have to do. Your performance might be
worthy of an Academy Award, but it will be worth it. How you
handle being discharged says a lot about you. Your employer may
be so disarmed by your coolness that she will reconsider her actions. If not, she will, at least, be impressed by your mettle.

2. *Ask for help in finding a new job.*   The best time to ask for
assistance in locating another position is while your boss is still
feeling remorseful about firing you. Discuss outplacement services or, if you work for a big conglomerate, ask for a spot in
another division.

3. *"Please, sir, I want some more."*   You don't have to act as
pathetic as Oliver Twist asking for more gruel, but in a businesslike fashion, do ask for more severance pay than you're being
offered. Being unemployed, after all, can be a grueling and expensive experience.

4. *In a nonchalant, matter-of-fact manner, inquire if you may
use your office and secretary while you job hunt.*   Jo Foxworth
reminds you that "You really will need them. Better to have a
crisp secretary answering your phone than a kid with a mouth
full of peanut butter sandwich."

5. *Pamper yourself for a short time.*   If there was ever a good
time to buy yourself a present, this is it. Get your hair done, have
a manicure, a pedicure, a massage—the works. You deserve it.
Splurge a little. Go to a matinee and enjoy a play you've been
eager to see. Indulge yourself with a short vacation. A long weekend might even be enough time to restore your shattered ego.
Whether you go on a vacation at all or how long you stay will, of
course, depend on how healthy your bank account is and what
sort of family responsibilities you have.

6. *Don't take your own firing personally.*   Genevieve Bazel-
mans, a partner in the outplacement firm of J. J. Gallagher Associates, discusses how women react to getting fired:

"Both men and women take it badly, but women hold on to
those feelings longer, because they take it more personally. Often
they've marched a long and solitary road. And the women we
work with are high achievers; they haven't lost too often. When
they do lose their jobs, they feel they have failed. . . . Women
haven't learned to lose as gracefully. It takes them longer to re-
establish their self-esteem. A man who loses his job already is
thinking about the next one. He isn't thinking, "I've failed."

Women question their abilities, instead of simply regarding the situation as a bad match."[9]

7. *Get your good-old-girls (or boys) network geared up.*   Start calling everyone you know to tell them you are available for employment. You *don't* have to give them graphic details of your dismissal. Betty Lehan Harragan, author of *Games Mother Never Taught You,* feels that you should "never say you were fired. Getting fired is an anachronism straight out of the female language. Cessation of employment with a specific company is alluded to in the usual business jargon, such as:

"Left by mutual agreement—Means your salary checks stop at the end of the month.

"Staff cutback—We don't have any work we want to give to this person."[10]

8. *If you're really organized, you'll have a plan of action before you are fired.*   Jane Trahey in *Women and Power* suggests being prepared before doomsday arrives. "Instead of wildly trying to gather in two hours evidence that you've been at work eight years, why not systematically keep the good things you've done in envelopes with the month and year carefully recorded on it? Each month you can take the envelope home and stash it away. . . . Keep a list of the people you meet—what they do and how they could be helpful to you if you need them. Keep in touch with them. . . . While you have access to electric IBMs have your secretary type and Xerox your résumé. . . . This service will save you time and money should you get the gate. . . . If you have hiring power, try to use only one headhunter. That way they owe you."[11]

9. *Kill them with kindness.*   No matter what rotten (expletives deleted) your former employers are, don't broadcast it to the world. It makes you appear small-minded; worse than that, it may make potential employers wonder what you might eventually say about them.

10. *Make your swan song end on a happy note.*   Don't leave in a huff; rather leave them laughing. Being such a good sport might actually get you back in the old ballgame at a later time. Maybe someone someday will recall your grace under fire and offer to hire you back at a pretty fair salary.

Venting your wrath at your boss today may embarrass you tomorrow if you have occasion to work with him again. Therefore, restrain the urge to try out your new karate chop on the Lord High Executioner. You may regret it someday.

Most employers are afraid of firing women for sexist reasons because women now have some legal clout. However, if you do feel you have been discriminated against because you are a woman, get thee to the Equal Employment Opportunity Commission (EEOC). Firing based on sex discrimination is clearly against the law as covered by Title VII of the 1964 Civil Rights Act. If you are uncertain as to whether your case is one of discrimination, check with your lawyer, the Human Rights Commission, the Commission on the Status of Women or, as I mentioned, the EEOC. Remember that the law is on your side.

READING THE HANDWRITING ON THE WALL BEFORE YOU READ THE PINK SLIP IN YOUR MAILBOX

The signals that you are about to be fired are often as clear as road signs. In order to map out a smart plan of action before your road to ruin becomes a fait accompli, here are some warning signals to watch for that clearly say, "Caution, danger ahead!"

You suddenly have no work to do. Liz White, an advertising copywriter in a Charlotte, North Carolina, agency noticed that her staggering workload was dwindling down to nothingness. The cause, unfortunately, was not that her supervisor had noticed poor Liz was overburdened; he was farming out her work just before he put her out to pasture.

Your boss and co-workers used to pop into your office frequently for a casual chat. Now your office is so lonely you find yourself having meaningful dialogues with the file cabinet. Be warned: Nobody likes to hang around with a doomed person. If no one says "Hello" to you, you can bet it won't be long before you can tell your job "Good-bye."

People don't return your phone calls. If people within your company who used to call you back immediately now never answer your phone calls, your number could be up.

Your boss is treating you as if you were the Shadow. If your boss acts as if you don't exist, "there may be evil lurking in his heart." If his door always seems shut to you or if when he con-descends to see you at all, he spends the entire time on the phone or dictating to his secretary, you're in trouble. He may be treat-ing you as if you are invisible because he knows soon you will disappear for good.

Your name is dropped. A not very subtle sign is noticing that your name is deleted from the Monday morning memo or that you have *not* been invited to attend the weekly staff meeting.

You hear a rumor. Sometimes it pays to listen to the rumor-mongers in your office. Much of what you hear at lunch or the water cooler is true. Often management leaks the news of your dismissal so you will take the hint and quit on your own.

Office musical chairs. Suppose you come to work one morn-ing and feel as though you are suffering from amnesia. You walk into your office and there is someone else sitting at your desk. The intruder coolly tells you that she has taken over your terri-tory and that your office is now located on the first floor. Hoping that this is just a bad dream, you stumble down to the first floor, which turns out to be the basement, and realize you have been kicked down to what looks like a former broom closet. The mes-sage is clear: you are being pushed out.

SHOULD YOU FACE THE MUSIC OR SAVE FACE BY QUITTING BEFORE YOU GET FIRED?

Okay, so you're no dummy. The warning signs are ubiquitous, but you loathe the idea of getting fired. Should you quit?

Before you do anything, ask yourself how much you really want to keep your job. If you really love your work, perhaps the thing to do is to try to save your job rather than to save face. Make an appointment with your boss. When you sit down to talk, be pos-itive rather than negative. Don't look woebegone and moan, "What am I doing wrong?" Instead, appear very self-assured and in-quire, "How can I do my job even better?" Ask for specific sug-gestions. Tell your boss how much you like your job and that you will try to follow her advice in every way.

She may be so impressed with your initiative and so relieved that the lines of communication are open, that she may decide to keep you on.

FIRE SIDE CHATS

Suppose, now, that the inevitable has happened: you've been fired. Is there anything good that can come out of this miserable experience? The answer is *yes!* Believe it or not, you can learn a lot from being fired. Now I am not exactly known as a modern-day Rebecca of Sunnybrook Farm and I thought Pollyanna was the silliest story I've ever read. Some people have even gone so far as to call me a cynic, but I still believe there are some good things to be gleaned from getting fired. "Like what?" you ask skeptically.

Well, for one thing, it's a good learning experience. Stop feeling sorry for yourself and sit back and ask yourself a few questions. Maybe you were in the wrong field. Maybe you were actually doing something wrong that you can improve upon before your next interview.

Jane Trahey suggests the following constructive retrospection: "Were you ill-equipped for the job? Wrong background? Could you have taken some courses that might have helped? If you stay in this field, should you take them now? Were you too inexperienced for the job? . . . Was your system planning inadequate? Did you fail to meet goals? Can you see gaps in your performance? Did you lack ideas? . . . Were you well liked? Were you dependable? . . . make your exit a growing experience as well as a going experience."[12]

More conversations with yourself.   Don't kid yourself about why you got fired. Get to the heart of the matter. Here are some more reasons why the ax might have fallen and how you can learn from the experience:

Was it really your fault?   Maybe you shouldn't take the firing personally because it may have had little to do with you. I once worked in a major advertising agency where an entire department was called together at 10:30 A.M. and told not to come back after lunch. Generally, this type of mass execution means the company has lost a big account or project and has had to do some drastic budget cutting. If you are part of this type of canning, it probably had nothing to do with your ability. The same thing applies to a shakeup after a corporate merger or when a new boss is hired and brings in his own staff. Your learning experience in this instance is that business can be a brutal classroom. However, in this case, you can at least consider yourself an innocent casualty.

Personality conflicts. If you were a Bella Abzug working in a Phyllis Schlafly-type company, there was bound to be a problem. Most companies tend to retain and promote certain executive types and to reject others. You may have been fired because your personality did not fit into some narrow-minded stereotype. Or, even if your personality blended well with the company's, perhaps it did not mesh well with your boss's. In either case, you can now give up trying to be somebody you're not and begin to search for an employer who will value you as you are.

Getting fired actually can work to your advantage. Getting fired actually may be just the incentive you need to get fired up. Maybe you are so mad that you are determined to work harder than ever to show those misguided folks just how wrong they were. This type of "creative hatred" can be a great incentive for success. Just so you think I am not merely a cockeyed optimist, let me leave you with the following story:

Mary Tyler Moore—yes, even Mary Tyler Moore—was fired once.

The story is told that Mary, after playing many episodes as a sultry secretary on the television series "Peter Gunn," asked for a raise. Instead of getting more money, however, she got fired. Well, we all know that this story has a happy ending. Mary went on to co-star in "The Dick Van Dyke Show" and, of course, captivated the heart of America as Mary Richards in "The Mary Tyler Moore Show." Who knows? If Mary hadn't gotten fired, maybe she would have faded into oblivion by now. What a terrible thought for us all.

So you see, getting fired can be a positive experience. You may not end up as the star of your own TV series, but you just might become the star of your own life. So don't get discouraged; instead Fire Away at something new.

2
Checks and Balances

DEALING WITH MONEY, RAISES, AND PROMOTIONS

"The making of money simply is not a sex-linked skill. Women can and are turning it all around. We are discovering for ourselves the challenge—and the joy—of money."
Paula Nelson

Money is power. So if you still believe that talking about money is somehow not ladylike, then you had better turn in your briefcase and go back to baking chocolate chip cookies—which, in these days of double-digit inflation, you may have to start selling on the street corner. You may have been raised to believe that "nice girls don't discuss money," but believe me, there's nothing nice about being paid less than your male cohorts. All the strides we have recently made in the business world will be as nothing if we can't feel the gain in our pocketbooks. Money talks and, if you really want to get ahead, you had better start listening!

Dr. Estelle Ramey, a leading feminist and endocrinologist (who, incidentally, is powerful and highly paid), has some well-coined phrases on this important subject. "Power to me is the ability to essentially control one's life basically in economic terms, because I am convinced that the control of the economic base of a life is the *sine qua non* of the control of every other aspect of a life."

Money—A Capital Idea

"Money means space, freedom and privacy. It buys everything from first-class plane tickets to living space to property to go to when you have to get away from people."
Cheryl Tiegs

"Honey, I've been rich and I've been poor. And rich is better."
Pearl Bailey

So how about it? Are you getting paid what you are worth so that you can spend part of every day in transatlantic calls with your Swiss banker principally discussing your interest? Have you recently gotten such a substantial raise that you have invested in a small gold mine? Was your last promotion so impressive that you personally flew over and bought your own Saudi Arabian oil field? Are the perks afforded you by your company so lavish that you have your own Lear jet and a private suite at the Ritz?

Or, are you, on the other hand, making so little money that you are living in an apartment that Ratzo Rizzo would shun? Perhaps you hope you will perform your job so brilliantly that a raise will automatically come your way? If so, you're probably also still waiting for Santa Claus and the tooth fairy to show up! Do you emulate Nancy Drew and sleuth around for clues to see if you are making as much money as your male (and female) colleagues? Or do you guard your paycheck as if it had the only known combination to Fort Knox? When someone asks you how much money you make do you clam up like an oyster?

Do you use your expense account to your advantage, or are you so frugal that you only used it once to buy an important client a Big Mac? (And then were you worried that people would think you a spendthrift?) Do you look forward to reading your company's financial reports with all the thrill and anticipation you would in getting a series of rabies shots? Are you still carrying around that outdated equation from your old arithmetic teacher that "girls are lousy at math"? If you still believe this poppycock, you can calculate your chances of getting to the executive suite are pretty slim.

Are you accepting euphemistic titles instead of cold cash? Your mother may be impressed that you are now the Executive Assistant instead of the Assistant Executive, but try seeing how much clout that has in the supermarket.

Your attitude about money may be holding you back. Some women will never confront their limiting timidity about money, but for those of us who have had our consciousness raised on this subject, let's now be conscious of how to get raises.

Nice Girls Finish Last

Before we look at the checks and balances of our working day,
let's briefly explore some of the myths and misconceptions we
have about money. You might ask what difference it makes if you
know about all of these alleged money hangups? Good question!
By the same token if your slip was showing or you had spinach in
your teeth, wouldn't you want someone to tell you before you
went in to ask your boss for a raise? The situations are similar in
that you may not be aware that you're carrying around some
problems that could damage your bargaining power. Remember
Pogo's profound observation, "We have met the enemy and he is
us."

Appearance vs. Reality, one of Shakespeare's favorite themes,
is another aspect of the problem. Even though you may know
exactly what you are doing money-wise, if the men you work with
consider all women to be hopeless dingbats incapable of playing
Monopoly, you will still be in trouble. So that you'll know what
you're up against, let's explore the following myths and realities
and see if any of them apply to you.

THE MYSTIQUE OF MONEY IS A MISTAKE

Being afraid of lucre is ludicrous. It's a lot more frightening to
be underpaid. If you want to spend your time being afraid, become terrified of poverty, because that is really scary. As Estelle
Ramey points out, "The fact of the matter is, the aphorism that
'money doesn't buy everything' is a non sequitur, because poverty certainly doesn't buy dignity. And it sure doesn't buy love."

How can this fear of money hurt you at work? Take the case of
Barbara Panghurst, a dynamic real estate broker, who was offered an executive position in the Cleveland home office. She
was delighted with the opportunity until she discovered that she
would have to make financial reports and that figures would figure heavily into every aspect of her new job. She turned the
opportunity down because "I never was any good at math." Well,
we all know that's nonsense. She was just acting out a female
stereotype and in doing so, ensured that her career advancement
added up to zero.

If you want to get to the top, then you had better take into account the fact that you need to know about MONEY. As Jane Trahey put it, ". . . the jobs that require math and finance are power jobs." Before you turn down any promotions for a job that requires math, compute the damage you are doing to your career. Perhaps you did indeed flunk Math 101, but so what? You can take a refresher course in accounting, finance, or whatever you need to get ahead. I'll bet you seven shares of common cents it will help your career.

Trahey also suggests that you "make a friend of an accountant, a bookkeeper. While you're latching on to techniques . . . try to relate what you're learning to the business you're in. You'll be amazed at how differently your job will begin to look to you. And you'll be pleasantly surprised at how quickly you start to be noticed. Money is power. But knowing about money is power, too."[1]

Nice girls don't talk about money; but then nice girls don't have to work for a living.   You were taught that it is gauche to talk about money—right? Well, that may be true if you are wallowing in the green stuff like the Vanderbilts or Rockefellers and can afford to be tastefully discrete. But for the rest of us mortals, it is fine to discuss money. More than fine, it is a good idea. An heiress probably doesn't have to worry about whether it is nice to ask for a raise, but you may. As Beverly Lannquist, vice-president, Investor Relations, United Technology, points out, "Women are embarrassed to ask for money because they don't feel that they deserve it. They have a really negative image of money; it is sort of inbred into our conditioning that nice women don't ask for money."

Keep in mind that one of the reasons we were raised to believe that it "wasn't feminine" to worry our "pretty little heads" about money is because this belief is a way of keeping women submissive and in their place. Next time your childhood conditioning makes you reluctant to ask for a raise or promotion, ask yourself who deserves it more than you do? "No one!" you say. Now, there. Isn't *that* a nice feeling?

I've got a secret.   I was raised in a household where I was taught that sex and money were not to be discussed in public. But how some things have changed in recent years! As you know, all too many people now blab about their sex lives to anyone who will listen. Money, however, is still an intimate, not-to-be-discussed topic. For instance, it is not uncommon to read the lurid memoirs of a person who would be deeply offended if you asked her how much money she makes. It is now considered chic to show someone your new French tickler and even describe in detail how you used it last night. God forbid, however, that you leave the price tag on it for the world to see. Now that would be sinful!

Money, in other words, is the last taboo. Men are generally better at sharing their financial secrets than women are because until recently they have had more secrets to share. A woman might be willing to disclose a bargain she found while shopping, but she will usually shut up when asked about salary and other "personal matters." In your case, this type of close-mouthed policy will clearly hurt when you try to find out if you are making as much money as your cohorts. This is no time to imitate the Sphinx; learn to speak up about money!

The cookie jar mentality.   Many women were raised to think small. That is not to say that they are not terrific money managers since, in most households, women do indeed literally hold the purse strings. However, women often spend hours trying to save money on a box of whole wheat cereal rather than taking a longer-range view and worrying about the price of wheat on the commodities market.

Can this small-time mentality hurt our careers? The answer is "yes," and in a big way! Many top executive men know where they will be in five years and exactly how much money they will be making. If you, on the other hand, are only trying to figure out if you are making enough money to buy a new dress, you are being shortsighted. You may pass up the right promotions, or accept titles instead of cash if you don't know precisely where you are going. Leave small-time thinking to small-minded people; you, my dear, should be headed for the Big Time!

Portrait of the woman executive as a young cheapskate.   Your frugality is showing! Maybe you have the·adage, "A Penny Saved is a Penny Earned" stitched in needlepoint hanging in your living room. Fine! Keep it there. But don't bring this philosophy into the office place. Women have a reputation for being penurious. You may think these charges are a cheap shot, but cheap is the image you have in the outside world. Think about it before you start screaming "Untrue!" Wasn't that you I saw last week splitting hairs over who owed the extra penny at lunch? How about that scant tip you left at your business lunch (on an expense account, no less)? It would have made the unreformed Scrooge look like the last of the big-time spenders. Aren't you the one who rides the subway to save money instead of hopping a cab? You are certain not to impress your colleagues by your thrifty ways if you arrive at your meetings looking rumpled from the rush hour.

Can your tightwad ways hurt your market value at the office place? You can bet your bottom penny they can. Thinking big about money is a prerequisite for many top corporate jobs. If your boss is afraid that you would be too cheap to spend the necessary money for an important lunch with a top client, then you might get demoted back to the person who gets the coffee and doughnuts. So, if you want to persist in this dollars-to-dough-nuts mode, nurture your cheapskate ways. If, on the other hand, you want to join the big leagues, learn how to think big.

The dizzy dame image. Saving the worst for last, I regret to remind you that women are often considered so scatterbrained that they couldn't handle money properly if they had the late J. Paul Getty himself as their money manager. This offensive Blondie image is unfortunately the way many others see us. We are reduced to caricatures who are obviously not to be trusted with anything larger than a weekly allowance. This portrait of the woman as a blithering financial idiot is, of course, absurd.

Paula Nelson explains in *The Joy of Money* why we have been so badly typecast: "Between woman's appointed societal role and her achievement of financial success lies a barrier so effective that it kept us passively accepting the role of money moron for centuries; the money mystique, based on the myth that financial expertise is distinctly unfeminine."[2]

Naturally, if women in general are thought to be "money morons," they will not skyrocket to the top of companies. This myth must be dispelled. We have to overcompensate and *never* give anyone a chance to exclaim, "Ah ha! Just as I suspected, the woman's a dingbat when it comes to money." If you are intimidated by financial matters, mum's the word. Tell your therapist or your accountant, but not your boss. As I said earlier, take some classes if you need to learn more about money.

We are now presumably freed from our inbred money problems, or, if that is too simplistic, we are at least aware of what they are. So let's get on with the enriching subject of how to make money.

It's some of your business. Do you know what salaries people around you are making? If you don't, in this case, what you don't know definitely can hurt you. The gap between what male and female co-workers make could equal the Grand Canyon. In a recent survey conducted by the Women's Bureau of the Employment Standards Administration, U. S. Department of Labor, it is revealed that the earnings gap between men and women has nearly doubled in the last two decades. Put yet another way, women earn, on the average, fifty-nine cents for every dollar men earn. Jo Foxworth embellishes these depressing statistics: "In 1979 . . . women college graduates had a median income of $10,861 while their male counterparts got $17,891. Among executives paid $25,000 and up per year, only 2.3 percent were women, and among managers, 5 percent."[3]

So forget all this nonsense about not talking about money or about being too polite to ask what anyone else is making. The hidden paycheck helps aid discrimination, and you, my dear, may be being discriminated against.

Beverly Lannquist feels that many times it is a woman's own fault if she is paid less than a man. "I really feel strongly that most women put a lower evaluation on themselves than men do. Many more women are willing to accept a lower salary than men would for the same job. You can't only blame the organizations; half the problem is the women themselves." In this case, silence is definitely not golden. You don't have to be silver-tongued to speak up, but if you don't you'll have no one to blame but the silent woman (to wit, yourself).

SEEK AND YE SHALL FIND—THE MYSTERY OF THE HIDDEN PAYCHECK

The first clue in discovering what those around you earn is so elementary that it would make even Dr. Watson blush. You merely ask. Don't be coy, be direct. Inquire what your boss, your subordinates, and your colleagues make. Don't stop there. Sleuth around other companies that do similar work. Don't expect to get this information for nothing. Be ready to tell others what you earn.

If your co-workers seem reluctant to share their salary secrets with you, you might suggest putting a batch of paycheck stubs (or pieces of paper with salaries written anonymously on each) in a hat, then add up the total and figure out the average.

Another suggestion is to find an executive search organization and consult with them when looking for a job or seeking a raise. Salaries are no secret to headhunters.

There are more suggestions for finding out what others in your field make. Start checking out the want ads in newspapers and trade journals. Ask around at various state and private employment agencies. Don't forget to bring up the subject of salaries at the next meeting of your trade or professional organization.

Finally, if you discover (or even have strong suspicions) that you are a victim of sex discrimination, run—don't walk—to the nearest Equal Employment Opportunity Commission. It's important for you to know that the law is on your side. You have paid your dues, so it's time to get paid what you're worth!

If You Find You Are Getting Paid Compliments Instead Of Money, Then It's Time To Ask For A Raise

The importance of asking for a raise.   Maybe you are one of those happy-go-lucky types who could survive selling snow tires on a desert island. Perhaps you don't mind budgeting those meager pennies you take home every week. "After all," you may say, "I love my job and my needs are few." Is it still important to ask for a raise? The answer is *"Absolutely!"* and for several reasons:

First, you've probably always been underpaid compared to your male colleagues.   If you followed my advice and found out what those around you earn, you should know by now whether your salary is fair or not. However, you can bet your last red cent that most men have been playing the "asking for more salary" game all along. As a result, if you have been sitting around being "good old uncomplaining Mary" and have merely accepted whatever raise was offered, you probably haven't kept pace with your male counterparts.

Second, what you get paid today will determine what you get paid tomorrow.   If you are still shrugging your shoulders and thinking "I get paid *pretty* well, so maybe it's not worth going to the trouble of asking for a raise," maybe you had better think a little further. If you have been settling for less than you're worth, you could be hurting yourself more than you realize. Keep in

mind that your future raises and benefits will be influenced by
how much money you are making right now. Over ten years'
time, your "so what?" attitude could cost you thousands of dollars.

Third, there's the specter of inflation. With the price of
everything escalating every time you turn around, inflation is pretty
hard to ignore. However, many women are so pleased to be getting any raise at all that they don't take into account that their 6
percent pay increase is a pittance in these days of uncertain inflation. A raise that doesn't take into account your new rent or mortgage payments often is no raise at all—it's a loss. Keep your salary sights high—you'll be glad you did the next time you step
into a grocery store.

*Fourth, if you accept less money, you are hurting women
everywhere.* Remember that good-old-girls network we've been
trying so hard to establish? Well, if you work for less money than
a man, you are hurting yourself and damaging women's salaries
everywhere to boot. We're all in this together, and whether you
like it or not, you are your sister's keeper.

*In a similar vein, needing the money shouldn't influence your
decision to ask for a decent salary.* Let's say your husband is in
a league with the late Aristotle Onassis and you are working just
for the fun of it. Or perhaps you are single, but get trust fund
checks in the mail every month that would keep most of us up to
our eyeballs in oil wells and gold nuggets. Is it important to ask
for more money? Of course! If you are only working for "pin
money," the rest of us are going to get "stuck" with your meager
salary! The primary reason you deserve regular raises is that you
are owed reimbursement for the job you were hired to do and do
well.

When I was a partner in an advertising agency, my partner,
Charles, suggested that we get paid according to our needs. His
reasoning went as follows: since I had a husband who was making
a good living, I should get less than the other partners. I point-
edly reminded him that we were *not* working for the Salvation
Army and were not getting paid on a sliding scale according to
need. I was doing an equal share of the work and didn't feel like
playing Lady Bountiful by being penalized because I happened
to be married!

Finally, if you aren't working for money, you won't be taken seriously. Have you ever been to a cocktail party where people were playing the "what do you do for a living" game? Did you notice that the women who answer, "I am the president of the League of Women Voters" or "I volunteer at the Cancer Society," aren't usually taken seriously? I have known these women. I often have been in their place. There's no denying that they frequently work harder than most paid workers. But time and time again, I've seen people ignore these "volunteers," and why? Simply because they *don't get paid.*

To sum it up, we do indeed live in a society where we are measured by our net worth. Whether we like to admit it or not, the more you are being paid, the more valuable you are deemed. If you don't command enough respect to get paid what you are worth, you won't be taken seriously. Accordingly, your executive clout will be seriously diminished! As Samuel Johnson so eloquently put it: "No man but a blockhead ever wrote except for money." The same holds true for working women. Why would anybody want to work and not be rewarded for it? Why indeed?

RAISING THE QUESTION

Okay, now you know the importance of asking for a raise. But, how do you go about it? Consider the following ideas:

Psyching Yourself Up. Athletes like Billie Jean King psych themselves up before any tournament, so take a tip from her and use it for your own racket. Put yourself in the proper frame of mind and look objectively at your assets. To get the proper perspective for the big confrontation, ask yourself the following questions:

1. How indispensable am I to the company? You obviously will have a better leverage if you are the only human alive (or at least in your company) who can use the Monte Carlo method for computer simulation solutions.

2. How much will it cost them to replace me? If you can coolly rattle off figures telling how expensive your replacement would be, you will be giving your boss an extremely persuasive reason to grant you the raise.

3. What if my boss says no? Will you want to quit on the spot? Can you get a job elsewhere? What is the market like now?

The time to ask yourself these questions is *before* you ask for the raise, not during the middle of negotiations.

4. *Is my company flush now or did they just file for bank-ruptcy?*

5. *How well does my boss like me?*

6. *What have you done for me lately?*   Look at it from their viewpoint and ask yourself, What's in it for them? Have you helped raise sales, cut costs, make important client connections? The more you have done for the company, the more they are likely to reward you.

THE GOOD-TIME GIRL—GOOD TIMING IS IMPERATIVE WHEN ASKING FOR A RAISE

Pick a time when you are feeling relaxed, prepared, and in a great frame of mine.   Obviously, if you have never had an original thought before noon, wait until afternoon to approach your boss. Likewise, if you have just ended a love affair and are feeling like Camille, you are probably not cheerful enough to undertake this important task.

Only approach your boss at his best time of day.   Carefully assess his mood. He obviously will not be feeling like Santa Claus if he has a terrible hangover or his baseball team just lost the pennant or he just had a miserable lunch with his counterculture daughter who informed him she has finally gotten a job as the West Coast representative for The Cocaine Connection.

Pick a relaxed time.   If the entire company is in an uproar trying to get out an annual report, this is *not* the time to ask for a raise.

"Bear" in mind that you will do better when your company is feeling "bullish."   Pick the time of the year when profits are at an all-time high if you want to get the best reception. *Choose your prime time.* You'll get better ratings if you ask when you are the superstar of the company, say, after you have completed a very successful project and people all around are still singing your praises.

The Actual Confrontation—Gearing Up For Battle

"Men are never so tired and harassed as when they have to deal with a woman who wants a raise."   *Michael Korda*

1. *Be prepared.*   What's good for the Boy Scouts is good for you. Dr. Sharie Crain in *Taking Stock* suggests that you "make a list, over an extended period, of all your areas of responsibility, the specific duties you perform, and how you allocate your time. Try to establish that, since your present salary was established, you have taken on additional responsibilities and performed them well and have become a more valuable and well-trained employee of the company. It is a fairly good general rule that the more important you can make your job appear, the greater the compensation management will feel it deserves. If you have made specific contributions . . . cite these when you talk to your boss. Try, if possible, to quantify the results you obtained, because most businessmen don't speak English, they speak arithmetic."[4]

2. *Have the salary negotiations somewhere other than your boss's office.*   Try to remove your boss from his own turf. You will feel more in charge if you are sitting in your own office, the conference room, or, best of all, outside the office atmosphere altogether. Ask your boss to lunch or for a drink. You can best weather the storm if you control the "rains." By regaling him with your low-pressure approach, you may get your due.

3. *It helps to have a good figure.*   Don't stammer and stutter like a foolish schoolgirl. Rather, have all the facts and figures in front of you and remain cool and collected. Know exactly what you are talking about. Determine in advance precisely how large a raise you want and how much this will cost the company by the hour, month, and year. Your boss may be so impressed by all this homework that he may figure you do indeed deserve a raise.

4. *Practice makes perfect.*   Since this may be the most important speech you ever give, make it reflect well on you by practicing beforehand in front of a mirror.

5. *Don't sell yourself too cheaply.*   Remember that you are involved in a bargaining game. Therefore, a certain amount of theatrics is an expected part of the show. Think of these negotiations as an important poker game with your salary (and ultimately your life-style) at stake. Be prepared to raise, pass, and bluff and don't ever take the first offer you receive without some bargaining. If you fold your hand too easily, you risk ruining your bluff. Your boss will feel that you would have settled for even a cheaper figure.

6. *This is no time to be a low brow.*   Think of the "high" as the limit. Always ask for more than you realistically expect to get.

Women, because of the conditioning reasons we have discussed, have tended to put too low a price on themselves. As Beverly Lannquist explains, "Most women who are in business today were not brought up to think of themselves as possible competitors in a man's world. This makes us less sure of ourselves, less willing to stand up in a fight. The major mistake I've made has been not to ask for enough money. I don't do that anymore."

If you go in hoping to get $25,000, keep in mind that your boss may have been thinking more in the neighborhood of $30,000. Remember, you can retreat from too high a figure, but you'll have a hard time recouping your losses from putting too low a price tag on yourself. Besides, your boss might start reassessing his opinion of you if he thinks you have a low market value. He might even wonder why he hired you in the first place. In other words, make certain that "The Price Is Right."

7. *Silence can be an effective negotiations weapon.* Maxene Fabe, a New York author, recommends "pausing for a long time before answering when a salary figure has been mentioned. Nothing unnerves an employer more than a long, pregnant pause. Some really skilled salary negotiators say that each second you are silent raises your salary a notch."

8. *Never hand down an ultimatum.* If you force the issue, you risk making your employer furious with you. If you make the threat of "a raise or else," your new "mad money" could be gone forever and so, for that matter, could you.

9. *Be diplomatic.* This is *not* the time to point out that you have always thought that your boss was a real drip and that he could use a new deodorant. Don't damage his pride. Make it easy for him to say yes.

"FREEDOM'S JUST ANOTHER NAME FOR NOTHING LEFT TO LOSE"

Suppose none of these tactics seem to work in your case. There are some last-ditch efforts that you can use with caution. Be aware, however, that you will have to travel at your own risk, because if you miscalculate, you may end up traveling to the unemployment line.

Making him an offer he can refuse. You might coolly inform your boss that you have received a better job offer elsewhere.

This move will give you leverage, since who in his right mind would want to lose a trusted employee like you? Right? Well, maybe. Be prepared, however, for your boss to give you his "I'll-miss-you-around-here" shrug and ask what day you'll be leaving.

The third-party negotiating method. Paula Nelson suggests that "you let it be known through your boss's secretary or some other key employee that you've had another offer and you 'don't know what to do about it.'. . . If he or she is a good, loyal type, and you yourself are a valued employee, the word will get out, and you'll get your raise, for one reason: 'The boss won't want to lose you.' "

This technique could backfire on you since your boss could be delighted with this leaked information. He might take the news that you've gotten a better job offer as the best thing to happen to his company since they put white wine in the water cooler. As Nelson warns, this technique should be used "only if you've been a 'good and faithful servant.' If you haven't you could end up feeling very embarrassed—and unemployed."[5]

P . . . . You're Promotable

If you think you'll get promoted because A . . . you're adorable, B . . . you're so beautiful, then Gee . . . you're sure gullible!

It's typical of our upbringing that many of us are too passive and that we wait for things to happen to us rather than making them happen. A job isn't like the old junior high school cotillion where a woman sits around waiting to be asked to dance. The business world dances to a different and more aggressive tune altogether.

Similarly, don't believe that old saw that doing a good job is its own reward. It will be a rare day when, by being true-blue and loyal, a promotion will automatically fall in your lap.

It pays to advertise. Let's suppose for the moment that you're doing a terrific job. But it's not doing you one bit of good if you're the only one who knows it. So stop sitting around and start becoming your own public relations agent. Here are some ideas:

Be very visible. Take on special projects that your boss and other higher-ups will notice.

Give speeches.

Get your name in print. Anytime you do something important,

write a press release (or see to it that your company's public relations office does it for you).

Join trade and professional organizations. Try to get a leadership position as soon as you can.

Don't be shy about any of your accomplishments. Make certain that your boss has a copy of any clipping about you and knows exactly where you are speaking and what new organization you are now leading. By being in the public eye, you are helping the company; you certainly deserve to be rewarded for this.

I can vouch for the effectiveness of these "Advertisements for Myself." When I had an advertising agency, I wrote press releases announcing all the awards we had won. I was also a vocal member of many advertising clubs and a frequent guest speaker in the community. Even though I was my own boss, advertising paid off. I was offered exciting and prestigious jobs throughout the country.

Don't keep your ambition a secret. Your boss is not a mind reader; maybe he thinks you love it where you are. Therefore, tell him that you want to get ahead and ask his advice on the best way to do so. Even though women are really making their mark in the business world, many men still have the old-fashioned image of the stereotypical woman who is not totally committed to her career. Your boss may think that you will work only *until* you get married or start a family. Set him straight by letting him know that you are interested in a career and not merely in a job. If you have never before told him, make it clear now that you are willing to travel, relocate, work weekends, or whatever it takes in your company to get ahead.

KNOW WHAT THE "PROMOTABLE QUALITIES" ARE IN YOUR COMPANY. THEN DEVELOP THEM

Obviously the traits that would make you chairman of the board of a record company are discernibly different from those that will make you a principal in a conservative banking firm.

Look around you. What are your company's unwritten rules? Are you more likely to become a top banana by remaining one of the bunch or by standing out from the crowd?

Alice Bessman, a real estate agent, found that in order to get ahead at her Atlanta realty office, "I was expected to get to work at the crack of dawn. Our founding father, a wise old owl, believed fervently in the adage, 'The early bird gets the worm.' I couldn't have disagreed with him more since my favorite maxim is 'Late to bed, late to rise.' I also knew, however, that it was important for my job advancement to put in an early appearance. It nearly killed me, but I dragged myself in every day at an hour that I had previously only heard about."

Maybe in your company the only way to curry favor is to wear purple socks on Tuesday or to wear a pair of monocles. To find out what is important, keep your eye on successful people around you and imitate them.

Audition for the part. If you know of a new job coming up, find out as much about the position as possible. Then strut your stuff in front of your boss by actually making a sales presentation of why you feel you are the best person for the job. If the boss doesn't seem terribly enthusiastic about your chances, ask why. Perchance you need to take some classes or get other special training. Let it be known that you will be delighted to do whatever is necessary (within reason, of course) to get the job.

Reviewing the situation. Sharie Crain advises that "if you have gone more than a year without a raise, a promotion or any indication of how your boss feels about your performance, it is important that you take the bull by the horns and ask for a performance review. Many supervisors are timid about telling employees what their weaknesses are and suffer in silence, muttering to themselves because you do not meet their expectations and silently punishing you by withholding promotions. Obviously, you can't satisfy their expectations if you don't know what they are, and a request for a performance review may give your boss the courage to speak out. It will also reinforce his perception of you as someone genuinely concerned about progress in her career."[6]

Always be on the alert for other jobs. Even if you now have a job that is the envy of all you meet, don't get complacent. There may be an even better opportunity right around the corner. Browse through the classified section of the Sunday paper and peruse the job market section of any trade magazines that you take. Keep abreast of any new jobs opening up in your company. Make certain your good-old-girls (and boys) network is up-to-date so you are informed of interesting jobs that come up.

When is a promotion not a promotion? Beware of becoming

a casualty of "The Patricia Principle" (the female version of the Peter Principle). A promotion in which you are promoted to your level of incompetence may be a demotion, not a promotion, sister. Let's say, for instance, that you are a copywriter to end all copywriters. Nobody has turned such nice phrases since the days of P. G. Wodehouse. Suddenly you are promoted to Creative Director where you don't do much of your own writing and have to manage other people. You hate the job and are consequently lousy at it. Is this a promotion that will do your career any good? Perhaps it will, monetarily and prestigiously; creatively, however, it may make you downwardly mobile.

Be careful of being kicked upstairs as the token woman. Because of legalities, companies have had to become more subtle in their discrimination techniques. They frequently promote a token executive woman and keep her hidden away in the corporate closet. When anyone charges discrimination, the company boys can cite their female senior vice-president. As Amy Greene, president of Beauty Checkers, puts it: "Many corporations practice total tokenism. They figure 'okay I've got one [a token woman]; she's a genius, she's marvelous, but let's keep her out of sight.' They only trot her out when it's company time."

Gracy Causey, of Charlotte, North Carolina, became her company's symbolic woman. She was given a vice-presidency, a sumptuous office, and absolutely nothing to do. She was so bored that she had sent all her Christmas cards by mid-July.

The upshot is that you should be wary when offered a better position. You just may be getting promoted to a dead-end job of no importance!

Title Waves

Pam Lee, a market research analyst for a cosmetics firm, told me recently of the fancy new title she had just been given in her company. She was bursting with enthusiasm. I felt somewhat like a cad when I asked her how much extra money she was making. "Thirty dollars a month," she answered sheepishly. Well, how about added responsibility? As she thoughtfully replied no to this question, she realized that she had been had!

It's easy to be caught up in the excitement of a glamorous new title, but believe me—you are better off keeping euphemistic epithets to a minimum and money to a maximum. Impressive appellations may wow people at cocktail parties, but they never buy anything tangible at the grocery store. So never be satisfied with merely a title; expect more compensation or more responsibility to go with it. If you see only titles coming your way, get out of there before you are caught in the next Title Wave. Beverly Lannquist did that very thing. "I left Manufacturers Hanover because of money. I was made an officer early, which was supposed to be a great honor, and then they told me that they could not give me the minimum officer's pay per year because it would have been too big a raise."

BE CAREFUL THAT THE FRINGE BENEFITS DON'T PUT YOU ON
THE FRINGE OF BANKRUPTCY

Don't be lured into accepting a job only for the terrific extras you are offered. There is certainly nothing wrong with good retirement plans, stock options, and so forth, but make certain they aren't accepted in lieu of salary or responsibility, but rather in addition to them. As Richard K. Irish so eloquently put it, "Where I work, we have one fringe benefit . . . cold cash . . . and it sure buys a lot more than all your corporate benefit programs!"[7]

Getting The Perks That Are Coming To You

Toni Priestly, a lawyer who started with a prestigious Seattle law firm several years ago, was telling a group of her associates that she had almost missed an important meeting because she had been unable to get a taxi. A male colleague looked at her incredulously and asked, "Well, why don't you use the company car?" Toni felt like a complete fool since she had not been aware that there was such a thing as "the company car."

So that an experience like Toni's doesn't become your road to ruin, make certain you know all the perks that are available to you. And how do you find out what extras should be coming your way? The answer is simple. *Ask!* When you first take a job or receive a promotion, and the salary negotiations have been completed, ask what perks you can expect. They vary greatly from company to company. Possibilities include lavish expense accounts, company charge cards, the company car, a reserved space in the parking lot, access to a particular country club or executive club, the use of a particular hotel or apartment while traveling, bonus pay, vacation time, insurance, health benefits, stock options, pension plans, child care, and exercise facilities, to name several.

If you can't get all this information from your boss, trot on down to Personnel and ask what's coming to you. I have personally found it a wise idea to ask for a job contract. In it everything should be spelled out completely: your duties, your salary, and, of course, your fringe benefits. People usually act startled by this request, but I insist upon it. If it causes too great an uproar for you, then the next best thing is to write a letter yourself to your boss or personnel office, stating in great detail everything you understand your new job is supposed to include. In this way your letter will be on file for all to refer to if you are denied anything you have been promised.

Once you know what your perks are, you should by all means use them! Not only will you save time and money, you will save face. If you don't take advantage of what is rightfully yours, you won't be taken seriously by your peers and, in the perverse way things happen, could jeopardize your career.

Not Handling Your Expense Account Properly Could Cost You Your Job

Cathy Gallaway, a public relations specialist, is still chagrined when she tells the story of her faux pas that occurred when she was sent to a convention by her Memphis-based firm. "I was on a full expense account, but I really didn't quite realize that I was supposed to use it. Here everybody else was wining and dining potential clients while all I ever did was buy a friend a sandwich in a tacky little sandwich shop. I guess I thought people would think I was a spendthrift if I took anyone out to a really classy restaurant. Boy was I wrong! When I got back home and my boss looked at my expense account, he was furious. He told me I hadn't done my job properly since I hadn't entertained enough clients."

As we discussed earlier, women's cheapskate ways can be very expensive mistakes for their careers. Keep in mind that expense accounts are not perks like a Christmas ham, but are indeed legitimate business expenses. They can be intimidating at first, but the lack of them is even more intimidating. I had my first expense account when I was in my early twenties and was working for American International Pictures. The first day I was a little concerned about overspending, but I quickly realized that using my expense account was a major part of my job: I was expected to treat amusement editors to lunch, take film stars to dinner, and stay in first-class hotels. It took me no time at all to adapt to and to lead the good life afforded by my expense account. So forget your upbringing; it may be bringing down your career. If you are discussing a huge business deal, you certainly don't want to take your client to a Taco Bell. And if by your stingy ways you make your company look like Jack Benny, you probably won't get laughs—and you may just lose an important account.

Keeping detailed records is the first and last rule of expense accounts. According to Sally Rubio, a Santa Fe accountant, the following rules should be taken into account: Expenses which your company will accept as legitimate should be spelled out by your employer in detail, well in advance of your trip or business meeting. That way, you will know the limits of your spending, and you won't be stuck with any expenses that your employer considers frivolous.

The common expenses that most employers will reimburse are:

1. Travel expenses to and from business meeting locations. This includes air fare, car rental, taxi fares and tips, travel insurance, and, most often overlooked, business use of your personal automobile. Whenever your own car is used for business, the mileage must be recorded, and most employers will reimburse at the IRS standard rate of 20½ cents per mile. You would be surprised how quickly mileage adds up.

It is important to note that if you detour from your business trip route for personal reasons, you should pay for any additional costs out of your own pocket. For instance, if you are on the way back from a business meeting in L.A. to your place of employment in San Francisco, and you decide to run by and see Aunt Maude in Denver, any additional costs must be incurred by you.

2. Entertainment, which includes meals and tips at which business is discussed, and other entertainment, which may include tickets to special events with a business or goodwill purpose in mind. In this area, it is always best to get an okay from the home office first, since the line between business and pleasure is rather thin.

3. Lodging, including your hotel and related tips.

4. Other expenses may include supplies or equipment rental or purchases necessary to conduct your business, passport or visa costs, foreign currency exchange losses, and under some circumstances, secretarial services.

If you are planning on taking your spouse on a business trip, check with your employer first, and you may find that, as is the case with many companies, your firm will pick up your spouse's expenses as well.

When attending a costly business meeting, most companies will advance money for expenses, based on estimates of what the trip will cost. Also, airline tickets can be purchased well in advance of departure, allowing for reimbursement in advance of the trip. This cuts down on the cash outlay required by the employee.

If you find that spending your own money is unavoidable (i.e., you have approached your employer and he cannot or will not cover travel and/or transportation, including meals and lodging), then you may deduct those expenses under "Employee Business Expenses" in the adjustment section of your 1040 tax form. This is where good record keeping is a must, and why you should record all travel expenses you incur, not only those your employer has promised to reimburse.

Getting The Credit That You Deserve

Just as Rodney Dangerfield "don't get no respect," women often don't get the credit they deserve. Until recently women were looked upon as erratic and not altogether clearheaded.

Probably you are aware of the vital importance of credit worthiness in the personal sphere. But have you also taken into account how important a good credit rating can be in the business world? If you haven't, you could be headed for big trouble. Consider the case of Susan Travis, who leads a hectic and exciting life as a sales representative for a Texas computer firm. She does a great deal of traveling and business entertaining and consequently relies heavily on credit cards. Imagine her embarrassment when she was taking an important client out to dinner in a French restaurant and a haughty waiter informed her that they could *not* accept her credit card since she was over her spending limit! The client, chivalrous, but not terribly impressed, ended up picking up the check. It turned out that Susan had been so busy traveling that she hadn't submitted her credit card bills to the company in quite some time. They had piled up, she had continued charging ahead, and the result was this embarrassing evening.

Many companies expect you to spend your money on a trip or dinner and then get reimbursed afterward. Therefore, if you don't have a credit card you will have to use personal cash reserves.

Similarly, let's suppose you have just gotten your first important job and want to take out a bank loan to buy an impressive new wardrobe. If you have never had credit in your own name or don't, for some reason, know how to go about this procedure, you could damage your career.

Therefore, since the issue of credit affects your professional as well as your personal life, let us look at some credit problems and try to decide how to handle them. First of all, did you know that it is against the law for women to be discriminated against in credit matters? This is a fairly recent gain. It wasn't until the passage of the Equal Credit Opportunity Act in 1975 that women were given clearly defined credit rights and could no longer be denied credit on the basis of sex or marital status.

In this plastic world we live in, a good credit rating is worth its weight in imported oil. How do you make sure yours is a good rating?

A CREDIT TO YOUR GENDER

If you don't have a credit rating, shame on you! But don't despair. Here are some tips on how to establish credit that I think you'll get a charge out of.

To get a good credit rating, go into debt. This advice isn't as incongruous as it first appears. It turns out that the best way to establish credit is to take out a bank loan. Mary Elizabeth Schlayer and Marilyn H. Cooley in *How to Be a Financially Secure Woman* suggest that you take out a short-term loan to run 90 to 180 days. "You want it to establish credit. That's the only reason."

Once you've borrowed the money, don't go out and buy a plane ticket to St. Moritz. You've taken out a loan to establish credit, not to go on a joy ride. Schlayer and Cooley suggest that "if you're extremely susceptible to temptation, put it immediately into a savings account, even in the same bank. Go straight from the loan officer to the teller's window and tuck the money away, safe from your hands."[8]

Once you've borrowed the money, don't forget about it. As a matter of fact, pay it back before the due date. If you have asked for a short-term loan of ninety days, repay it in sixty to seventy days. You might have to pay a small penalty for your efficiency, but it will be money well spent. Just think of it as a small price to pay to insure an excellent credit rating.

"NOBODY KNOWS MY NAME"

Once when I was young and foolish, I tried to rent a car without a credit card. I was on a business trip in California and naively offered to leave a hundred-dollar bill as collateral. The rent-a-car people were nonplussed. I might just as well have suggested leaving my old wornout tennis shoes. To add insult to injury, I was under twenty-five—the magic age for credit car rental trustworthiness. Needless to say, I was turned down flat. I ended up taking taxis everywhere, which was very inconvenient. From then on, I took a cue from American Express commercials and realized that no matter how important I thought I was, without a credit card, "nobody knew my name."

Another good reason to have credit cards is because without them, you virtually don't exist. If you have ever been without a credit card and tried cashing a check or establishing your identity in almost any city, you know that you might as well forget it. If Descartes had lived today, his famous saying would have been, "I charge, therefore, I am."

How do you know which credit cards are best for you? Deciding is not an easy task these days. Cards vary from state to state according to law and the competition of each marketplace. To make an intelligent choice, you must become an informed consumer. Every financial institution wants you to select their card, so make them work a little for your business. Ask questions about credit cards, beginning with ones offered by your own bank. Laura Fitch, vice-president of Commercial Lending, Bank of Santa Fe, suggests asking the following questions about credit cards:

◊ How much is charged (usually an annual percentage rate)?

◇ On what amount are charges assessed, the beginning, closing, or average balance?

◇ Is there a free ride period?

◇ Is there any annual fee?

◇ Will you have cash advance privileges with this card?

◇ Will you have privileges with out-of-town banks?

Ask these questions of your bank, credit union, savings and loan, and, of course, the credit card companies themselves. Ask your friends and fellow employees which type of card from which type of institution they have preferred and why. Once you've done all this sleuthing, taking all the information into consideration, choose the card that is best for your career and life-style.

YOU ARE WORTH MORE THAN YOU THINK

I thought I knew everything there was to know about obtaining credit until I read *The Joy of Money*. There I discovered how to determine my Net Worth, which is, as Paula Nelson explains, "a financial photograph of the dollar-and-cents side of you." Handing your banker a copy of your net worth makes you appear very professional and is an excellent selling tool to use when applying for a loan. I discovered this recently when asking for an increase on my MasterCard credit line. I presented my net worth to my banker, who was apparently so impressed that I got a much larger credit line than I had requested. Just so you can use your net worth calculation as a bankable tool, I will literally take a page from Paula Nelson's book to show you how good you really look.

"The following form is simply a suggested outline; you will undoubtedly have special additions or deletions to make. Your calculation should be done formally, preferably in ink. And I suggest that that you keep it in a permanent folder, tagged 'Jane Doe, Net Worth,' or 'Doe family, Net Worth'—and be sure you date it. This is, by the way, the same type of calculation a company makes at least once a year. So you are, in effect treating yourself like a corporation, as you should."[9]

SUGGESTED NET WORTH CALCULATION

Net Worth Statement

of

_____

Date

ASSETS	(Fill in Amount)
Cash on hand	$_____
Checking accounts	_____
Savings accounts	_____
Corporate profit-sharing plans—money now due you	_____
Marketable stocks (lower of cost or present market value)	_____
Money you have lent someone	_____
Life insurance (total cash surrender value)	_____
Bonds, including U.S. government	_____
Real estate	
Home (at market value)	_____
Investment properties	_____
Syndications	_____
Automobile(s), current market value	_____
Furs, jewelry, antiques, paintings (market value)	_____
TOTAL ASSETS	$_____

	(Fill in amount)
LIABILITIES	$_____
Unpaid bills	
Charge accounts	_____
Credit card accounts	_____
Taxes (payable in next 12 months)	_____
Insurance Premiums (payable in next 12 months)	_____

Rent

Installment contracts   _____

Loans: Banks   _____

    Savings and loans   _____

    Insurance companies   _____

    Credit unions   _____

    Car loans   _____

    Mortgages   _____

    House and other real property   _____

TOTAL LIABILITIES $_____

Summary of Net Worth Calculations

ASSETS $_____

LIABILITIES $_____

Net Worth (assets − liabilities) $_____

Learning How to be "Well-Bread"

I have barely scratched the surface of the myriad money matters that may affect your life. Since money is power, it is definitely in your best interest to find out more about this important subject. Some suggestions that you shouldn't find too taxing include:

Workshops. Our country is becoming workshop-oriented and, for the most part, this is great news. I have attended and, in fact, conducted countless workshops on Women and Money. If you don't know of any in your area, check with your banks, credit unions, women's centers, and other women's organizations. If you can't find anything useful, be resourceful and sponsor your own workshop through one of your professional organizations. Keep in mind that there is a wealth of information out there.

Universities. Many continuing education classes offer courses on Women and Money. There are, of course, the classes that I mentioned earlier that deal with accounting, finance, bookkeeping, or whatever is most relevant to your job. You can add a lot of class to your life by attending a few courses on money management.

Books.   There are some excellent books that address money matters in great depth. Besides *The Joy of Money* by Paula Nelson and *How To Be A Financially Secure Woman* by Mary Elizabeth Schlayer and Marilyn H. Cooley, two other books that I would recommend are: *Everyone's Money Book* by Jane Bryant Quinn and *Sylvia Porter's New Money Book for The 80's.*

"We women ought to put first things first. Why should we mind if men have their faces on the money, as long as we get our hands on it?"   *Ivy Baker Priest*

3

Judging a Book by Its Cover: How to Be a Best Seller

SOME NOVEL WAYS TO PACKAGE YOURSELF

"And what authority even the creases in a suit can convey . . ."
Doris Lessing

Let's suppose that you are the most diligent worker this side of Ralph Nader and possess the business sense of J. Paul Getty. You're going to set the business world on its ear, right? Well, not so fast! You've left out one important detail. What kind of image do you convey?

If you think that your physical packaging isn't crucial to your success as an executive, think again. Creating a positive first impression is every bit as vital as your expertise as an executive. If you don't present an image that conveys an immediate sense of confidence, all the business know-how in the world won't matter.

But it's what's inside that counts, you protest. This may be true, but it's what's outside that shows! Look around you. With few exceptions, success comes quickest to those who look and sound like winners.

Suppose, for instance, that you and Mary Jones have exactly the same credentials and that both of you are being considered for a promotion. Perhaps, on the one hand, you don't devote much effort to how you look, sound, and act because you think these should be considered petty details as long as you are doing a good job. Perhaps Jones, on the other hand, has a polished, businesslike appearance, is very smooth, and presents an excellent first impression. Who will get the promotion? Most likely, Jones, not you. But you can learn to keep up.

Maybe you believe that just being a competent worker is enough to get ahead. If so, you probably still believe in the tooth fairy. Competition is often fierce in the business world and it's the accouterments you bring to the job that separate the women from the girls.

So what do you need to know in order to present a terrific-looking package to the world? Business manners, for one thing. Class, taste, and savoir faire are the marks of a good executive. In this chapter we will discuss some ways to improve your business etiquette. Also, are you aware that there is a new etiquette in the business world? If not, read on and learn when the new etiquette is appropriate, and when it is smarter to bow to the old etiquette.

What about emotions at work? Is your career being slowed down because you reinforce men's image of the "overemotional" woman? We will take a calm and logical look at this subject and find ways to avoid giving men (and some other women) reason to say, "Aha! She's acting just like a woman."

And what do your speech and body language say about you? Have you listened to yourself lately? Do you know the art of good business conversation? Is your public speaking so good that you're ready to go on the lecture circuit? Or are you terrified of getting up in front of ten people to speak? On a similar subject, how's your telephone etiquette? Do your telephone manners have the ring of authority about them?

Finally, take a look at your office. What does it say about your importance as an executive? Do you know what type of office is considered powerful? Are you cognizant of some of the absurd office power games being played? When should you redecorate your office? Is it attractive, comfortable, and inviting, or does it look like the company's storage room?

Each of these aspects is an important part of your total physical presentation. Some concern themselves with tiny details that you might have overlooked, but when it comes to putting your best foot forward, it's backward to overlook anything. First impressions are generally created by little things, sometimes the most picayune of details. But, small as they are, they can loom large in building the right business image.

So give yourself a little polish so you, too, can be a best seller.

Business Etiquette

Rudeness in any aspect of life is intolerable. However, in the business world of late, brusque, curt behavior is often worn as proudly as the Red Badge of Courage. It shows you have arrived. You are an important person, and therefore it is incumbent upon you to be rude.

I'm in total agreement with Janice Handler ("A Plea For Good Manners," *Savvy*, December 1983) who is "launching a one-woman 'back to basics' movement—a plea for good old-fashioned manners. By manners, I mean the stuff your mother and your eighth-grade teacher taught you; the rules about being on time, being gracious on the telephone, and being kind to others. Not only has there been a degeneration of manners in recent years, but it is accompanied by a kind of perverse pride in rudeness, as if one has scuttled along the fast track much too quickly to have wasted any time acquiring a certain polish on the way."

After dealing with just one too many insensitive, arrogant business colleagues, I often yearn to be a Jane Austen heroine where civility is all-important.

There's a method in your manners. Not only is it humane and sensitive to be polite; it's also very practical. Since so many people behave with the charm and finesse of Attila the Hun, you, by acting politely, will stand out from the crowd. The business world, needless to say, has its share of boorish louts. However, I am happy to report that the majority of the top corporate women that I interviewed were gracious, exceedingly polite, and in general represented the epitome of good business etiquette.

Good business manners, in essence, indicate professionalism and class. Unless you are in a decidedly cloddish profession, your polished business etiquette is bound to make a favorable impression on others and help you get ahead in your career.

It's practical to be polite. Good manners are a sign of respect and courtesy to your employees, employers, and co-workers, and they have their practical side: it is well known that if people are treated politely, they will respond in kind. In addition, they will generally be much happier and productive if they are being treated, not as robots, but as human beings.

PLEASE CONSIDER SOME OF MY TIPS ON BUSINESS MANNERS.
THANK YOU.

Because your business etiquette is such an important manifestation of your overall package as an executive, it's a good idea if your gift-wrapping looks as if it came from Neiman Marcus rather than from the dime store. Here are some examples of business etiquette that are important to me. You are welcome to use whichever ones suit your office decorum:

1. *Rise to the occasion.*   When a visitor enters your office, stand up to greet him or her with a smile and a handshake. It's a nice way to make the person feel welcome and get the meeting off to a good start.

2. *Have telephone calls held when a visitor is in your office.*   There is nothing ruder or more distracting than trying to conduct business with a person whose ear is permanently attached to a telephone. This phoney mannerism does *not* have a nice ring to it.

3. *Try to return phone calls even if you don't yet have an answer.*   Nothing is more frustrating than waiting for someone to "get back to you." Negligence is not the sign of a good executive, and people will be impressed with your courtesy if you call them back.

4. *Be on time.*   Nothing makes a poorer impression than a person who is chronically late for appointments. If an emergency occurs and you can't be somewhere on time, always at least call, apologize, and explain your situation.

5. *Please and thank you may be the most underused words in the business world.*   Make certain that they are an integral part of your vocabulary.

6. *If you make a commitment, keep it.*

7. *If you are wrong, apologize.*   Don't overdo it and don't be self-deprecating in the process. A simple "I'm sorry" will suffice. Since these words are also suffering from underexposure, they will be appreciated.

8. *Get into the habit of writing thank-you notes for business lunches, dinners, and drinks.*   Even if the social event was in the line of duty, a thank you, although not de rigueur, is never out of place and is certain to impress the person being thanked.

A FEW INTRODUCTORY REMARKS

Since the subject of introductions is one of the most crucial parts of business etiquette, I will deal with it at some length.

Introduce yourself—"Think before thou speakest" Cervantes. Janet Stone and Jane Bachner suggest that introducing yourself is a type of "verbal résumé." "An effective thumbnail sketch of who you are is tough to invent on the spot, so figure out what to say in advance. Who are you? . . . A verbal résumé should include, at the barest minimum, your name and your reason for introducing yourself into the situation."[1]

Always introduce yourself with your first and last name, i.e., "Suzannah Smith" rather than Mrs. Hieronymous Smith, Ms. Smith, or Miss Smith. In a business setting, give your title if you have one (i.e., "I'm Suzannah Smith, marketing director of the Digital Widget Corporation.)"

Your opening line, of course, will vary greatly with the situation. If you feel that you should get right down to business, simply state the matter at hand: "I understand you are the leading authority in Chicago on digital widgets. Therefore, I'd like to discuss our product with you."

If the meeting is more informal, size things up. If you are dealing with bright, witty people, a clever opening remark might be in order. If you can tell that someone has spent a great deal of time designing his office, your first comment might be one discussing the attractiveness of said office.

The name of the game. Don't let someone play power games with your name. Titles among adults should be reciprocal. For example, it is one of the pet peeves of my husband who is a Ph.D. when a medical doctor introduces himself in this pompous fashion: "Hi Dave, I'm Dr. Frankenstein." He quickly makes his displeasure known when he answers, "Hi Bruce, I'm Dr. van Hulsteyn." The moral is clear. Do not allow anyone to first-name you unless you are first-naming back.

We have to start meeting like this—how to introduce others. If you have ever been in a situation where a group of business associates are talking and no one has bothered to introduce you, you know how a leper must feel. Not introducing people is the *height* of rudeness! If this happens to you, simply step up and introduce yourself.

Since you now know how awkward it feels not to be introduced, don't be an offender. You may happen to introduce two people who already know each other, but that's all right. It's better to err on the side of politeness.

Who's on first—who is introduced to whom? The etiquette books of olde have quite a lot to say about the proper way to introduce people. However, the rules and regulations on propriety make my head swim. While trying to figure out who is the "more important person," I picture myself asking the two people to stand there silently while I compare their credentials. Therefore, I am inclined to agree with Stone and Bachner, who feel "these conventions are ageist, sexist, classist, and deserving of swift death. Similarly, we feel uncomfortable with introductions that dwell on the individuals's rank, status or 'importance' in male institutions. Try to describe . . . others in ways that don't promote categories of 'who matters and who doesn't' or 'the somebodies and the nobodies.' "[2]

Let's shake on it. Always extend your hand after being introduced. Take the initiative so the other person doesn't resemble an umpire giving hand signals as she is wondering whether a handshake is appropriate.

Put some life in your handshake. We all know how pleasant it is to shake a hand that feels like a soggy piece of cold lasagne. On the other hand, this isn't the time to demonstrate your new bone-crushing judo hold. A firm two- or three-second handshake is the order of the day.

The eyes have it. While shaking hands, don't forget to make eye contact.

MORE WELCOMING TIPS ON SOCIAL GRACES FROM THE
GRACIOUS LADY HERSELF

No section on business etiquette would be complete without the following advice from Letitia Baldrige:

"The worst error anyone can make while on a business appointment is to stay too long. . . . Fifteen minutes is a good rule of thumb to use in deciding when to end an appointment . . .

"Don't relive personal experiences concerning a social occasion outside the office in front of others who were not invited. . . .

"Don't drop by another person's desk to chat just because you are not busy at the moment. . . .

"Don't borrow colleagues' telephone books, newspapers, pens . . . or any supplies without immediately returning them after use. . . . Executives who borrow reports and reference materials from associates should not forget to return them. . . .

"A woman should not fix her makeup and no one should do a hair-styling job on himself or herself at the desk. People of both sexes who are serious about their career do their primping in the rest rooms."[3]

REFLECTIONS IN A CORPORATE EYE—REMEMBER THAT YOUR
SECRETARY AND RECEPTIONIST ARE MIRROR IMAGES OF YOU

Perhaps you were at the head of your class in charm school and are still the quintessence of stylish splendor. Before you get carried away with your social graces, however, remember you are also judged by the company you keep. So take a look at your secretary and receptionist. Keep in mind that the first impression a person gets of a company (and hence the executive) is determined by the people he encounters first.

I don't know how many offices I have been to where my first impression was a gum-chewing receptionist who was dressed inappropriately (often in a skimpy halter). This person often looked as if I were boring her by my presence and getting in the way of the really important work of doing her nails. Many times such a receptionist would have cutesy stuffed animals and other inappropriate paraphernalia cluttering her desk. Male secretaries and receptionists are not immune from similar lack of courtesy and professionalism. If such a person is my *first* contact with a company, I will probably have *second* thoughts about the organization and the executive that I have come to see.

So although you may not be your secretary or receptionist's keeper, it is your responsibility to see that she creates a positive impression. After all, she's part of your physical presentation too.

OLD ETIQUETTE VERSUS THE NEW ETIQUETTE IN BUSINESS

The old etiquette in the business world is archaic. It's difficult for a woman to consider herself as an equal when all her male co-workers still deferentially hold doors open for her. There's a new game afoot today and to play it you need a whole new set of rules. The entire theme of this book is dedicated to the modern businesswoman, who wants the doors of the business world opened *to* her, not *for* her.

The new etiquette assumes an egalitarian atmosphere and is in essence a matter of *people* being courteous to other *people*. Common sense and sensitivity are the key words for the new etiquette. Let's look at some specific examples of how this works:

Stand up and be counted.   Show that you are democratic in your standards. For instance, when you enter the office of a male executive, he should rise to greet you. Likewise, when a male executive enters your office, you should extend him the same courtesy by standing up.

The new "open door" policy.   The new open-and-shut rule on this subject is to do what comes naturally. In other words, if you happen to get to the door of the boardroom first, you should open it for a fellow executive. On the other hand, if he gets there first, he should open it for you.

More handy advice.   Whichever man or woman is carrying fewer reports, briefcases, or packages should open the door for the other one. If you are really courteous, you might even offer to help carry some of the burden.

The elevator shuffle.   This isn't the name of the latest disco dance; it's the archaic practice of letting women in and out of elevators first. It has probably resulted in the maiming of countless office workers and certainly the loss of many productive business hours. So here is the new uplifting advice on how to handle this song-and-dance: Whoever gets on last gets off first.

Who's on first.   Ladies before gentlemen went out with bouffant hairdos and girdles. Now it's every man for himself (and every woman for herself). Marcille Gray Williams, in the book *The New Executive Woman*, has the following running commentary on this high-stepping issue: "Those with the highest status walk first. If you are hosting guests, then they always walk first, no matter who has the highest status. The remainder of the time, it makes no difference."[4]

SOME GROUND RULES ABOUT THE NEW ETIQUETTE

The new etiquette is simply a matter of common sense and egalitarian courtesy. There are times, however, when you must ask yourself how important this etiquette is to you and to your image. As much as we all want to be treated on an equal footing with men, it is wise to remember that the higher you climb on the business ladder, the more likely you are to encounter old-school men, trained from the crib to be gentlemen. These old-fashioned, chivalrous types may mean nothing demeaning by helping you on with your coat. Is it worth making a fuss over?

It depends. Look at the situation. If you make too much of such an issue, you may give the impression that you are more concerned with women's movement problems than you are with the overall functioning of your business team. Some old-world types would also consider it a lack of polish and good social graces if you were to harp on what they consider an insignificant matter. This could indicate to them that you would not be a good representative of your company in other social situations.

If, on the other hand, you feel that a man is being chivalrous for the sexist purpose of keeping you in your place, you should speak out. When it is obvious that he is opening the doors for you to show you that you are still the "little woman," then it is time to give him a "little lecture." Even in this annoying situation, it's best not to make a scene. Try to have a private discussion with the offender and explain how you feel.

A Rational Discussion of Emotions at Work

Let's face it, women. We have a bad image of being too emotional. Whether this image is fact or fiction isn't important; what is important is the *perception* that the "overemotional" woman exists. I will therefore try to remain calm as I relate parallel executive traits as seen through a myopic Double Standard:

◇ A businessman is aggressive; a businesswoman is pushy.

◇ He follows through; she doesn't know when to quit.

◇ He is careful about details; she's picky.

◇ He isn't afraid to say what he thinks; she's opinionated.

◇ He's a stern taskmaster; she's hard to work for.

◇ He exercises authority; she's tyrannical.

◇ He pounds the desk or slams a door, and he's being forceful. She raises her voice or slams a door, and she's being a bitch.

◇ He cries at work, and he is being sensitive. She cries, and she is being hysterical, moody, and unprofessional—"just like a woman."

Unfortunately, we've all seen examples of the above in action. I once worked in a movie production office where the male executive in charge had a disposition that made Idi Amin look like Albert Schweitzer. He had an ungovernable temper and left people shaking in the wake of his furor. Enid, a female director, who worked as his associate, was his antithesis—always calm, professional, even-tempered. However, one day as she was directing a scene for an upcoming movie, her headphone and microphone went out. Since there was no time for repairs, she took them off and started shouting instructions to the actors on the set. It was all in the line of duty. Her boss, remaining true to character, was his usual maniacal self.

Needless to say, however, the rumor immediately circulated, "Watch out for Enid today, she's hysterical." About her Stalinesque boss, nary a comment was made. As Jo Foxworth puts it: "Since people will be expecting you to 'act like a woman,' avoid any behavior that can be labeled as such."[5]

Let's look then at how men (and many other women) are expecting us to act and make certain we exasperate their expectations by *not* acting that way.

NO, THAT ISN'T JUST LIKE A WOMAN

Everyone doesn't have to like you. Many women, unfortunately, have been conditioned to believe that everyone has to like them. An executive position is not, however, a precursor to the Miss America Pageant, and at work you're not supposed to be concerned primarily with being "Miss Congeniality." For instance, when I owned an advertising agency, men often seemed surprised that I was not easily manipulated into doing what they wanted. One client put it to me this way: "You look like such a sweet young thing, but you are a tough businesswoman. Don't you worry whether people will like you?" Smiling, I replied, "I don't care if they like me as long as they respect me."

That, indeed, has been the credo of my working life. Now it so happens that most people find me quite likable, and I go out of my way to be pleasant. However, I don't care if everyone in the firm, including the janitor, is not crazy about me. Neither should you.

Handling criticism. Women have the reputation of taking

criticism too personally. Consider this example concerning Joan Goodman, a Chicago banking executive. Goodman was criticized by her boss for an error she made in handling a customer's account. Rather than accept the incident for what it was, she reacted very strongly. She felt threatened, as if her very value as a human being had been called into question, and feared that her whole career might be in jeopardy.

Goodman's example is typical of how some women respond to criticism. Sharie Crain feels that if we women fail at any work-oriented task, we often "identify our whole being with the single failure, thus losing our self-esteem and consequently our self-confidence."[6]

What should Goodman have done? Basically, she should have thought of the error and reprimand as part of a learning experience and profited from it. Her employer actually did her a favor in pointing out her mistake before it grew into a really grievous problem.

The underlying theme of this story is to learn to separate yourself from your work. When I had an ad agency, clients would sometimes throw my work across the room and comment, insensitively, "That's the worst piece of junk I've ever seen." I learned to let these comments roll off my back because I knew it had no reflection upon my worth as a human being (coupled with the fact that they had bad taste).

When you are criticized, figure out what you did wrong and how you can profit from it next time. Write down what you were criticized for, analyze the situation, and see how you can do things better in the future.

Confronting the issue. If a woman executive, say, comes to your office and begins to criticize you, here are some rules that you might follow.

◇ Let her know you understand the criticism by restating it in your own words.

◇ If she is being vague, ask for specific examples. Pin her down.

◇ Ask for advice on how she would have handled the situation differently.

◇ Don't forget your good business etiquette. Say you are sorry, if it is warranted. You might even close the meeting on a good note by thanking her for bringing it up.

Conversely, try the following:

◇ Don't be overemotional.

◇ Don't put her on the defensive: Don't say such things as: "Isn't that like the pot calling the kettle black? Look at the disastrous way you handled such and such. . . ."

◇ Don't overapologize or put yourself down.

YEA TEAM—LEARNING TO BE A TEAM PLAYER

Maybe you're getting tired of hearing the old cliché that women don't know how to be team players. One woman I interviewed, when asked about women's difficulty in understanding the team concept, scoffed, "Oh, that's been highly overrated. It's another relic from the way women *used* to be." Who knows? She may be right. After all, the number of sports programs for girls in schools is on the increase; girls are participating in Little League more and more, and women in record numbers are becoming important factors in the old ballgame.

Bear in mind, however, that we are discussing here the *perceptions* men have of a working woman. One such view is that she would rather be the star quarterback than sacrifice for the good of the team. A second is that she doesn't know any of the rules. Like all myths and clichés, there is an element of truth to these concepts.

LOVE THINE ENEMY

Women are pictured as not being able to work with people they don't like. Again, our conditioning is responsible for this undesirable business trait. In *The Managerial Woman*, Margaret Hennig and Anne Jardim discuss the differences in the way boys and girls are raised: "What boys learn that girls don't: flexibility, how to develop a style, a way of behaving that makes it simpler to get what one wants. . . . Boys learn how to put up with each other, to tolerate each other and to use each other to a degree that girls hardly ever find necessary. For men, friendship may be a valued outcome of interaction on the job. For women it too often tends to be a prerequisite."[7]

Unfortunately, I have seen women jeopardize their promotion opportunities because they didn't like the new man they would be working with. Take the case of Maria Martinez, whose field of expertise is solar energy. She was offered a vice-presidency with significantly more prestige and pay. This promotion, however, would have required her to work with a man she didn't care for. She was used to being friends with her business associates and didn't think she could work with a person she didn't like. Naturally, this decision cost her dearly, and from then on she was considered "not true management material."

So unless a person is really odious, grit your teeth and learn to work with him. There are plenty of people outside of the working world you can be friends with.

Crying Is Appropriate At Sad Movies, But Not At Work

For crying out loud, never cry at work! As Marlene Sanders, correspondent for CBS News, explains, "Crying is infantile and inappropriate business behavior. You should never do it. You must let your professionalism prevail."

There is nothing that turns off men or other women more than crying. Your veil of tears is considered manipulative and unfair and could cost you your job. Let's briefly examine why men react so negatively to tears while women have been trained from birth to use them to get what they want.

In our society women have been conditioned to cry. We have been taught that it's an acceptable way to play the game. We learned that some men will do anything to put an end to a woman's "sob story."

Most men, on the other hand, consider crying unmanly, and thus unprofessional. Even though men in the private sector are learning to be more sensitive, this type of "sensitivity" probably cost Senator Edward Muskie his political career after he cried in the 1972 New Hampshire presidential primary.

The corporate man, especially, considers crying in front of others an unacceptable executive trait for either men or women and the mark of someone you can't trust to make the right decisions.

LOOK BEFORE YOU WEEP

There is no better way for a woman to reinforce the overemotional image than by crying at the office. To make matters worse, it will probably endanger her career. Since this would be a crying shame, let's look at some things you can do when you feel the tears coming on.

The madwoman of the office place—why men prefer anger to tears.   Marcille Gray Williams tells the following story that illustrates why it is smarter to get angry than to get weepy. A high-powered female executive was severely criticized in public by a manager whom she respected. "I got so hurt and upset I felt like I was going to cry. I ran out of the meeting and held the tears in until I reached my office. I closed my door and cried, and then got hold of myself and marched into his office. I told him how unfair I thought he had been and how much he had hurt me.

"He said to me, 'I saw you welling up to cry. And I decided that if you came in here and started to cry I was going to fire you on the spot. . . . The fact that you went out and took care of it, and then came back in here with very logical, objective facts, and more importantly, the fact that you could articulate the problem you're having makes me want to deal with it and help you.' "[8]

Williams explains how all savvy businesswomen can learn a lesson from the above parable. "The attitude expressed by her boss is common to most businessmen. They would rather see you get angry than cry. So it's important that you learn to show anger. Most executive women have learned how to channel their feelings toward anger rather than tears, assuming it is necessary to show any emotions at all."

SOME TIPS ON HOW NOT TO CRY, BABY

Get mad, not sad.   As we have just discussed, anger is preferable to tears. So recognize the signals that a crying jag is coming on and learn how to channel these feelings into anger.

Anticipate situations which might make you cry and plan ahead of time on a course of action for dealing with them.   Spend some time alone, away from the office, and think about what types of situations, pressures, and people make you feel like crying. If possible, try to avoid these.

Recognize the signals for when you are going to cry.   Most of us can feel ourselves getting ready to cry—the lump in the throat, the quivering voice, the loss of control, the total vulnerability. When you recognize any of these symptoms, have a plan of action ready.

HOW TO VEIL YOUR TEARS

Take a break.   At the first signal of tears, immediately get away from the situation. No excuse is necessary, but if you want to cover your tracks, simply say, "I'll talk about this later." Or, if you want to be more specific, you might suddenly remember that you are expecting an important phone call or that you have an urgent appointment. You'll figure out the best way to "excuse yourself," but do get out of there before the first teardrop falls.

It's my office and I'll cry if I want to.   If you have complete privacy, sometimes the best thing to do is to let yourself cry. You certainly have a right to. Often it's the only way to release all the built-up tension and emotion. But do it alone! As Amy Greene cautions, "Go cry in the john or behind your closed office door, but never in front of the whole board!"

Pulling yourself together.   Some techniques:

◇ Have a glass of cold water. Rather than dampening your spirits, this is supposed to be a great pick-me-up.

◇ Have a relaxing cup of tea. This technique always works in Agatha Christie novels and other English literature. Maybe it will be just your cup of tea to stop the blues.

◇ Call your husband, lover, best friend. If there was ever a time for moral support this is it. Sometimes an encouraging word from a close friend can dry up the tears.

◇ Do something totally diverting. Read a mystery, plan your next week's dinner party, or call your travel agent to get her working on your vacation.

Repress your tears and cry when you get home.   Although this tactic isn't the greatest thing for your psyche (or your body), sometimes it's the best thing for your career. There are situations in which there really isn't the luxury of allowing yourself to cry—you're either too busy or can't find a moment of privacy. If this is the case, wait until you get home, then beat up pillows, cry your eyes out, and get it all out of your system. Sometimes this home remedy is the only solution.

Dealing with your period.   I know, I know. Women's menstrual cycles take a bad rap. We have all heard the classic lines such as, "A woman is too emotional during that time to *ever* be president." Or a male colleague may smirk if you get upset and say, "Oh it must be one of *those* days."

Since many men, and women for that matter, may expect you

to verify this female stereotype, *don't ever let them*. Women do, in fact, vary widely in how they react to their menstrual cycles. Some women are not at all affected, while others find they become more emotional and moody. If you fall into the latter category, plan accordingly. If possible, avoid scheduling stressful meetings during your period. If you have no control over these dates, at least take into consideration that you may be vulnerable during this time and cover your tracks. Get plenty of rest, and keep your spirits up by looking your most attractive.

Illegitimi Non Carborundi ("Don't Let The Bastards Get You Down")

The following advice can be applied to almost all of the situations we have been discussing, plus many others. It's all perfectly "logical," as Mr. Spock of "Star Trek" would say.

1. Don't act in haste. If you've had a disappointment at work or if your boss or co-worker is criticizing you, it's sometimes best to do nothing at all. Keep your objectivity and give the problem some perspective.

Gene Barnes, a New York public relations agent, advises: "Don't think about the problem for at least twenty-four hours. Let it simmer. In the meantime, treat yourself to a movie or play. Then the next day, figure out how you can persuade the person in question into giving you what you want."

2. Conservation of energy. In order not to have your own personal energy crisis, it's important to recognize which work situations are worth channeling your emotions into. You have to be smart enough not to put your good energy into a dead-end path.

3. The "write" approach. After an upsetting emotional scene, "get the facts, ma'am," rather than getting mad. Sit down and write an account of the whole incident in a cool, rational fashion just as if you were writing a business report.

4. I am a camera. If you picture yourself a budding Bergman, think of the event as if it were being filmed. However, make it cinema vérité; don't interject any of your subjective attitudes.

Next, record the feelings you had during the incident. Ask yourself if you want to act in this fashion during any such future experience. If you do not, then instead of fretting over what you did wrong, rehearse what your rational response should be. If you stage the scene in advance, you'll probably play the part correctly.

5. *Remember your long-range goals.* If you can't see the forest for the trees, then you're likely to be upset over every emotional setback at work. As Aileen Phillips, a public relations specialist, puts it, "Businesswomen need to learn to be more goal-oriented. If a person has goals and a way of reaching those goals, then she is not going to be upset by petty things that happen along the way. If you don't know how to set goals, attend workshops on objectives and goals."

6. *Learn to be assertive.* Many of us were raised to be overly considerate of others. Thoughtfulness is fine but being assertive is also a positive attribute.

If you feel like the office doormat, Robert E. Alberti and Michael Emmons, authors of *Your Perfect Right,* give the following definition of assertive behavior: "Behavior which enables a person to act in his own best interests, to stand up for himself without undue anxiety, to express his honest feelings comfortably, or to exercise his own rights without denying the rights of others."[9]

That certainly sounds like a person I'd like to work with. If it doesn't describe you and you'd like to become more assertive, sign up for an assertiveness training program. Contact your local women's center for how to find one. That's an order!

7. *Don't be the office therapist.* Many women play the role of the Dr. Joyce Brothers of their company. They are understanding and can always be counted on for a supportive shoulder to cry on. However, they're also probably being taken advantage of. For you to act as office psychologist would not be what you're getting paid for (unless, of course, that is your occupation). By the same token, don't be the office whiner; leave your cares and woes at home.

If someone keeps pestering you with personal problems, at first try making light of it. Say something to the effect that "I'm sorry, I'm not allowed to dispense therapy without a license." If this doesn't work, politely but firmly tell the person that you'd be happy to discuss personal problems outside of the office, but you feel it is unprofessional to let them interfere with work. If this still doesn't get the point across, simply say, "I'm busy working; I don't have time to discuss anything that isn't pertinent to my job."

8. *Keep your sense of humor.* To me, a sense of humor is a prime requisite for all aspects of the business world. Jo Foxworth concurs with this viewpoint. "The ability to see humor in dark corners is priceless and the gift for making other people laugh can add an enviable element to Management Style."[10]

9. *Remember, it's only business.* As I used to tell newcomers to my advertising agency, "If we stopped producing ads tomorrow the world won't come to an end. Is one ad really worth getting an ulcer over?"

10. *Running away from your problems.* I am, by no means, a representative of the President's Council on Physical Fitness; as a matter of fact, I'm a charter member of the Non-Runners' Club. However, it's a proven fact that physical exercise is one of the best ways to rid your body of tension. So the next time you start to get emotional, go take a walk.

11. *Workable relaxation techniques.* Since we can't always go swimming or jogging when we feel tense at work, we need to know some on-the-spot methods of relaxation. According to Dr. Sharie Crain, "The ability to relax at will when exposed to demanding and stressful situations is a characteristic common to most successful men and women."

Exercise good judgment and try these relaxation methods suggested by Crain: "Sit well back in the chair so that your body is fully supported. . . . Begin by breathing in and tightening the muscles all over your body. . . . Exhale and totally let go. . . . Next, take two or three long, calm, easy breaths, letting your abdominal muscles relax and rise as you do so. . . . Be aware of your neck muscles and how they feel. Turn your head from side to side so that you feel the tension and then the comfort as the muscle tension subsides."

Crain suggests this method for every part of the body and concludes that "if you practice this technique regularly and take it seriously you will find that you gradually become able to relax more quickly and for longer periods of time."[11]

I personally discovered this relaxation technique during my years as a yoga student and can vouch for its effectiveness.

12. *Whatever you do, keep your dignity.* No matter what the situation, try to be courteous and dignified. Anyone can swear

and blow up. It takes a very classy person to remain dignified under adverse conditions. You'll be certain to impress and bemuse your opposition.

FINALLY, KEEP IN MIND THAT WORK IS SUPPOSED TO BE FUN

I once had a job where my boss literally frowned upon any laughter, jokes, smiling, or other signs of pleasure in the office. Her puritan ethic philosophy seemed to be, "If you are showing any indications of having a good time, then you are obviously not working."

To her and other militaristic bosses, I politely say, "Balderdash." If you are going to do something at least eight hours a day, it had better be fun. Now granted, every day may not be like a perpetual vacation, but you should enjoy what you are doing or else not be doing it. Most extremely successful executives love their work. It's very hard to hit the big time if you hate what you are doing.

To love it, leave it. To make certain you love your job, leave it once in a while. Don't be a workaholic. Relax in the evenings and forget about work. Likewise, don't be a slave to your job every weekend, or you could be a casualty of the latest executive women's disease: stress burnout.

Get your job into perspective so it doesn't get to you. Be careful not to fall into the same trap that has ensnared men lo these many years:

Don't let your job become your entire reason for being. As Marlene Sanders puts it: "If you have nothing else in your life [husband, family, relationships of some kind], you tend to get overly wrapped up in your work and suffer from tunnel vision. Every aspect of your job becomes too meaningful. You need something outside to help keep you in balance."

Speaking Out—The Importance Of Speech In The Business World

Speech is one of the most important, and most underrated, aspects of physical packaging. Good speech skills are one of the major keys to business success. Here's what a voice of experience has to say on the subject: "What happens when we talk to people

exerts such a powerful influence that it can destroy—or reinforce—all our other positive attributes and achievements." [12]

Dorothy Sarnoff, author of *Speech Can Change Your Life*, also
airs her views on this subject: "The ability to speak confidently,
concisely, and convincingly is essential to anyone who is ambitious for business success. . . . If you are in business, your speech
image, which includes the way you look as well as how you sound,
will determine how far you rise." [13]

Now that you know the vital importance of this area, let's address some of the issues involved here.

SPEAK AND YE SHALL FIND—THE ART OF GOOD BUSINESS CONVERSATION

Swear off vulgarities.   Profanities never enhance your professional image.

Keep clichés out of your conversation.   'Tis "trite but true"
that clichés quickly become "old hat." I'll "bet my bottom dollar"
that you'll end up with "egg on your face" if your business conversation is cliché-ridden.

Don't speak psychobabble.   Wow, you've got to be really out-
of-sight to dig where I'm coming from. I mean, man, if you rap
like a Me-Generation Goonie, you'll probably be really far out in
the business world—far out in left field, that is.

Translation: Business people should use articulate, standard
English, not California Mellow-Speak.

Stick to the point.   I could go on and on and tell you why you
shouldn't ramble on forever (that incidentally reminds me of a
story about a Nash Rambler. It all started one day . . .) But the
basic point is, don't imitate Senator Filibuster.

Cultivate the use of a good vocabulary.   This is not to say that
you should be infatuated by the exuberance of your own verbos-
ity. Don't be an effete snob like Spiro Agnew or a pedant like
William Buckley. Do, however, add a three-syllable word now
and again. In an era when too few people speak eloquently, a
good vocabulary can be one of a businesswoman's most important
assets.

Watch it—your body language is showing.   If your mouth says
one thing and your body says another, most people will respond
to the gestures that speak louder than words. Be careful, there-

fore, what your body says about you. Janet Stone and Jane Bachner note that "Many women have adopted a completely self-effacing body language that might be called 'the invisible woman.' The message seems to be 'Don't take me seriously, I don't take myself seriously. In fact I'm not even here.' Those of us who are afflicted sit down in a way that won't offend the chair . . . and have been known to say 'Excuse me' when we walk into a wall."

So what's a body to do? Stone and Bachner are vocal on the subject: "Stand up straight, look people in the eye and quit fidgeting. . . . Force yourself to hold your head up (not cocked to the side) and just talk."[14]

Don't giggle or smile inappropriately.   Nothing diminishes your executive status more than girlish giggling. It's okay to laugh, but giggling is appropriate only for a slumber party of ten-year-old girls. If you say something forceful or unpleasant while smiling like a Miss America contestant, you will *not* be taken seriously.

Know what you are talking about.   Whether for a huge conference or for a one-to-one meeting with your boss, be prepared. Research all subjects so thoroughly that you'll never be caught off guard. This type of conversation is 1 percent inspiration, 99 percent preparation.

The voice of authority.   A pleasant, forceful voice is a tremendous business asset. Even if you are mouthing pearls of wisdom, you probably won't be taken seriously if you are speaking in a nasal, high-pitched, or whiny voice.

Voice improvement—Volume I. (Speak up, I can't hear you).   If you talk in a soft, sweet little voice, people will assume you are murmuring sweet nothings and dismiss you as powerless.

Just for the record.   To improve your voice quality, tape record a speech or a conversation you are having with a friend. Be warned, however. It can be a shocking experience! I have never known anyone who has listened to her voice who hasn't gasped, "Oh I couldn't possibly sound like *that!*" Well, unfortunately, Dear Reader, tape recorders, like cameras, don't lie! If you don't like what you hear, take a course in public speaking or read *Speaking Up* for tips on voice exercises.

Know when you should just listen, and hence keep your mouth shut.   As Edmund Muskie wisely points out, "In Maine we have a saying that there's no point in speaking unless you can improve on silence."

TELEPHONE ETIQUETTE

When calling:

Always identify yourself.   Beginning a conversation with "Guess
who this is?" might be considered cute by a junior-high student,
but it is decidedly unprofessional for you. My inclination when
someone plays "Guess Who" is to wonder, "Who cares?"

To avoid ambiguities, always give your name clearly and tell
what organization you're with. Then, pause. You could have a
wrong number or be talking to the wrong person.

Clear the other person's time.   Be polite. Ask, "Is this a con-
venient time for you to talk?" Obviously, most busy executives
aren't just nonchalantly lounging around their office, counting
their teeth while hoping that someone might call. They will appreciate your courtesy.

Make your own phone calls.   Having your secretary place calls
for you is showy and archaic. As Sally Richardson, subsidiary rights
director for St. Martin's Press, explains, "Having a secretary get
another person on the line first seems very pretentious. I make
my own phone calls to avoid all that nonsense." Reserve the use
of secretaries for times when you anticipate difficulty in reaching
your party.

Think of each phone call as a speech.   Phone calls can be serious business. Therefore, treat telephone conversations in the
same vein as you would a person-to-person encounter or a personal interview.

Be prepared—Make notes before and during the call.   Lois
Sherman, a Voice of America correspondent, always writes down
"in one sentence my opening line—i.e., what I'm calling about.
After I have delivered my opening line, then I stop and let the
person answer instead of rambling on."

Noteworthy advice.   It's also a useful practice to write down
all the points you want to cover in the phone call. During the
call, record pertinent points that the other person makes.

Don't talk too long.   Remember that in business conversations, "brevity is the whole of it."

Make certain you are talking to the right person.   Don't give
your brilliantly memorized presentation to the person who answers the phone. It may be the janitor or a wrong number. Make
certain you are talking to Mr. Big before you launch into your
speech.

Always have the name of the person you are calling.   People are always impressed if you call them by name. If you don't know who the president of the Parsimonious Pickle Company is, do some research in advance by calling the company and inquiring.

Don't gum up the works.   Chewing gum while talking on the phone never makes you appear bubbly; it's just a good chance for you to "blow" the conversation. Likewise, don't mumble.

Sound pleasant and human.   Carol Price, a graphics designer at Los Alamos National Laboratory, thinks, "It's important not to sound like you're an extension of the telephone and hence a machine. Your humanness should come through. People whose voices are extremely cold, remote, and show no emotion probably won't be very effective on the phone."

Voice improvement—Volume II.   Keep reminders by your phone to keep your voice at the right setting—not too low or too high. Also keep telling yourself that the word "um" has no place in the English language!

Leaving messages.   You should give your first and last name, your company, if pertinent, your telephone number and a brief and to the point message.

Always leave a message with the secretary if you can. If you can get a secretary or assistant on your side, there's a much better chance of your calls going through. Always treat them courteously and be candid about the reason you are calling. Don't try to be mysterious or refuse to give your reason.

How to deal with a secretary who acts as if she were guarding the pope.   If you can't beat them, join them. If you are getting nowhere with a surly harridan who resembles the phone operator Lily Tomlin used to portray, try being honest and direct. Inform her that you understand her situation and realize that it is her job to screen you out. If you have ever been a secretary, you might let her know you can identify with what she is doing. After you have (hopefully) won her confidence, tell her briefly why you need to talk to her boss and that your information or recommendations could greatly help the company. This approach implies that you could try to trick the secretary, but you've decided to trust her instead.

How to end the conversation.   Have a dynamic wind-up sentence prepared that clearly leaves an impression as to what you are going to do or what you want the person to do. Don't leave the person at the other end wondering what the call was all about.

When called:

Answer your own telephone, identifying yourself with your name. i.e., "Hello, this is Suzy Frump." Sound pleasant but businesslike. Rather than diminishing your importance, it will enhance your image if you act as your own answering service. As Betty Lehan Harragan explains, "I have discovered that the real status and competence of business executives is in inverse proportion to the number of people one must go through to reach the party. . . . Always call the highest ranking executive possible, preferably the president because he'll answer his own phone."[15]

Give the caller your undivided attention. Appear interested in what the caller has to say (unless he is trying to sell you an unwanted insurance policy or a ski chalet in Florida). Don't be barking orders to others in your office or carrying on any conversations with others. This is as distracting to the caller as talking to a frantic mother who spends the entire phone call screaming at her kids.

Call yourself up to see how your callers are treated. On a day off, call your office (disguising your voice if necessary) and see if you like what you hear. Is the receptionist cordial? Is your secretary friendly but efficient? You can learn a lot by being a mysterious caller.

There are no dumb questions, just dumb answers. Don't be afraid to appear stupid by asking pertinent questions. Gene Barnes voices her opinion on this subject: "I think one of the important things is that people are afraid to ask other people how they spell their names. They feel it is an indication that they are not paying attention, don't hear well, or are not quite as smart as they would like to appear."

Hold it. There is no place lonelier in the universe than "on hold." The only thing worse than being dangling there alone is being kept company by the ghastly sounds of Muzak. I'd rather listen to Edith Bunker sing! If you or your secretary must put someone on hold, don't forget them. I have made it a rule never to hold for more than three minutes. After this reasonable interval I may decide that perhaps I don't want to do business with this company after all.

On the other end, if you should be in the middle of a conversation and have to answer another call, say apologetically, "Excuse me, I'm going to put you on hold for just a minute" and

answer the other call. If the business of the latter cannot be finished quickly, say you will have to call back and return to the first
caller.

Pest control.   One of the drawbacks to answering your own
phone is that you are certain to get a few people who are wasting
your time. Here are a few lines to get them off the line:

"I have a long-distance phone call on the other line."

"I have an important meeting to attend."

"I'm late for a luncheon date" (a little suspect at 9 A.M. but
certain to get the point across).

In dealing with this pesty problem, don't forget your manners
(unless the offender is totally obnoxious). Sound polite, apolo-
getic, but firm.

My secretary/myself.   If you have a secretary or receptionist
answering your phone, make certain she creates *your* type of
image. Tell her *exactly* how you want your callers to be treated,
precisely what sort of messages you want, and the proper way to
answer your phone. A good secretary/receptionist or phone operator is worth her weight in Saudi Arabian oil. Treat her kindly.
Let her know that you think she is doing a terrific job and what a
valuable asset she is to you. (Of course, the same goes if your
secretary is male.)

Similarly, I am totally turned off by a secretary who is snippy,
filled with her own self-importance, and often rude. Worse yet is
one with a voice that sounds as if it belongs to the leader of a
tough New York street gang, or who is bored and chewing gum.
Listen to your secretary; she says a lot about you.

Talking back to an answering machine.   Ah! The answering
machine, one of the great joys of twentieth-century living. Many
people consider the answering machine the worst invention since
the motorcycle. However, answering machines can be conve-
nient, and, since they are a fact of life, you had better learn how
to talk to them.

If you have an answering machine: Make your recording cheerful
and welcoming. Many recordings sound as if the speakers had
just found out their business has gone bankrupt; hence they don't
exactly inspire confidence or exuberance. Other recorded messages sound a little daft, as if the speaker has been spending a bit
too much time talking to machines or to the furniture—anything
but another sensible human being!

If you are leaving a message with a machine: I know, you feel dumb talking to a machine, so you may want to hang up. However, that is rotten telephone etiquette, so don't do it. Likewise, unless you know the person really well, don't make some cute remark. They may not be amused!

Speaker of the House—Tips on Public Speaking

Some women would rather be condemned to a year's exile in Hackensack than risk speaking in public. Even the very articulate Gloria Steinem was once pathologically afraid of public speaking. She admits that "though I wasn't shy about bearding lions on a den-by-den basis, as journalists must do, the very idea of speaking to a group, much less before a big audience, was enough to make my heart pound and my mouth go dry. The few times I tried it, I became obsessed with getting to the end of each sentence without swallowing, and then obsessed for days afterward with what I should have said.

"And I would have remained silent, like so many women who were giving up on various aspects of their human abilities, if I hadn't been lucky enough to live through a time when a few women were beginning to figure out that the gigantic lack of confidence in females wasn't all our individual faults. A profound system of sexual politics was at work here.

"I say all this about speaking not only because it has been a major hurdle in my life, but also because it's a problem that seems to be common to many people who feel overly dependent on the approval of others."

However, Steinem conquered her fear of public speaking and you can too. Take heart from her example and her words: "Years of actually getting up in front of audiences have taught me only three lessons: 1) you don't die; 2) there's no right way to speak, only your way; and 3) it's worth it. A mutual understanding can come from being in a room together, and a sense of character and intention can come through the television screen that could never happen on a printed page."[16]

Tips that will make public speaking fun rather than terrifying include:

Be prepared.   This is not the time to try for Improvisational Theatre, unless you have the spontaneous talent of a Robin Williams. As Marie Hirst, a public relations expert, says: "If you accept a speaking engagement, do the people in the audience a favor and think about it beforehand."

Rehearse, rehearse, rehearse.   Go over your speech out loud several times and time yourself.

Don't memorize, familiarize.   Remember, a talk is not a poem you are memorizing for ninth-grade English. You are supposed to appear somewhat spontaneous. Do, however, rehearse until you feel comfortable with the speech and you know by heart the main points and their order.

Don't prop yourself up.   Beverly Lannquist suggests, "As soon as you can get away from crutches [like notes] the better, because they really detract from the effectiveness of the speech."

Tape your speech.   "The medium is the message," and if yours isn't coming across loud and clear, make a tape recording of your speech, study it, and keep practicing.

Mirror, mirror on the wall.   You don't have to be the fairest of them all, but do be fair to the audience. Observe yourself. Make eye contact and be sure your body language is saying good things about you.

Dress rehearsal.   Rehearse in front of a live body even if it's your two-year-old son or your senile aunt from Cleveland. Audience reaction is important.

Relax.   Very few speakers (outside of those inciting riots in South America) have gotten beaten up recently. So take several deep breaths and, to scare off panic, ask yourself what's the worst thing that can possibly happen? Barbara Walters noted that "A television performer friend of mine gets her composure together before a show by saying over and over, 'They can't kill me.' My own talisman is Abigail McCarthy's serene observation, 'I am the way I am; I look the way I look; I am my age.' "[17]

Speak slowly and lower your voice.   Speaking slowly allows you to calm down, and the lower your voice, the more confident you will sound.

Dressing the part.   Here are some tips from professional speakers:

Keep your look simple.   Solid-colored dresses or classic suits are your best bet. Avoid distracting busy prints and plaids that call attention to themselves and not to you.

The tailored look is always safe.

Keep your hair and makeup natural.

Avoid clanging jewelry.

Wear comfortable shoes. In other words, dress in the same sensible, attractive way as you would for an important business meeting. As always, the key word is common sense.

Don't adopt a modus operandi that is not you. As Marie Hirst puts it, "If you are a funny Irish lady [which she is], be that."

Know your audience. In advance, check the following points with your liaison, the person who is coordinating the arrangements for your talk:

Should the speech be serious or light?

Will there be two people or two hundred?

Is it a captive audience? (Translation: Will they be fired if they don't attend, would they rather be making daisy chains out of paper clips, or do they really want to see you?)

Will you be competing with Jack Daniels? A drunk audience can be anything but intoxicating!

How long are you expected to speak? Unless you have the charm of the late Hubert Humphrey, don't follow his speaking advice: "I've never thought my speeches were too long; I've enjoyed them."

Will your speech be publicized? Public speaking can help your career enormously, so make certain you get the publicity you deserve.

Do you know how to get to the speech site? I've been to many luncheons at which the speaker either didn't show up or arrived in a belated frenzy because he got lost and failed to ask directions. Don't let this happen to you.

Twenty questions. When writing your speech, anticipate questions from the audience and prepare to answer them. To make certain that there are indeed questions, try to line up a couple of people beforehand to ask some.

GROUP THERAPY: HOW TO DEAL WITH PROBLEMS WHILE
TALKING IN GROUPS

Speaking our minds might break up the old-boys network. Some men unfortunately still believe that women should be seen and not heard. As a result, mixed-sex meetings can be exceedingly unpleasant when men play dominance games.

Let's look at some of the techniques that many men use to

bring back "the silent woman" and discuss some ways we can speak up loud and clear to stop their actions.

When you say it, it's ho-hum. When he says it, it's brilliant.   Joan Howe, a professor of English literature, presented an important point about her research on Chaucer at a predominantly male faculty meeting. She might as well have been reading her grocery list, for all the attention the men paid to her. Just a little while later, a male colleague raised Joan's point (phrased, of course, in his own words), and one would have thought he had just discovered a new Canterbury Tale. His male cohorts listened attentively.

To avoid reliving this tale of woe, here are some ways you can handle this type of upsetting situation:

Speak for yourself, Joan.   Joan should immediately have claimed the idea as hers. She might have said something like, "I'm glad that you like my concept on Chaucer and have even taken the interest to embellish it. When I first mentioned it a half hour ago, I was afraid that nobody had heard me."

Gear up the good-old-girls network.   Such a moment is definitely the time for women to start supporting other women. (Of course, a sensitive man can just as easily come to Joan's rescue.) So if you hear a man stealing an idea suggested by a woman, speak up. "Gee, Rick, that's an interesting interpretation of the idea that Joan presented a half hour ago."

Interruptions: What to do if a man cuts you off in mid . . .   I was once speaking in an advertising seminar, holding forth rather profoundly, I thought. In the middle of one of my more erudite thoughts, a man cut right in and totally changed the subject. Now, cutting in may be proper behavior at the cotillion for changing partners, but it is *rude* and serves as a power play when done in mid-sentence of a speech. Therefore, I stood my ground and looked my opponent straight in the eye and remarked, "I'm certain we would like to hear what you have to say. However, I haven't finished yet. I would appreciate the opportunity to do so!" He was stunned by my audacity, but he shut up.

I now interrupt my story for a word of advice from Stone and Bachner: "Interrupt a man who is interrupting a woman. . . . When a man starts to interrupt, all of the women present should keep their eyes fastened on the woman who was talking. . . . Encourage the woman by reserving your attention for her until her turn is over. If you don't catch on to the fact that a man has usurped the floor until after the fact, you can still say, 'I didn't get all of what Amy said because Bill interrupted her. Amy, will you repeat what you were saying a while ago?' "[18]

Speaking of more ways women can help each other.   Support a woman when she speaks. At any type of meeting, if a woman has made a point, don't make her feel as if it has been lost in the black hole. In some way, recognize that she has indeed said something. You don't have to agree with her point, but at least acknowledge it.

The following support systems are suggested:

Encourage women to talk.   "Hold it a sec, Bill. I believe I saw Amy shake her head. Amy, did you have a comment?"

Provide one another with opportunities to speak.   "Cindy, you've had more experience with this than most of us. Do you have any suggestions?"

"Congratulate, thank and praise one another on good points."[19]

The Executive Suite

Obviously an office is an important part of your physical presentation. If you are seated out in the hallway or occupy the back half of the company's freight elevator, people aren't likely to be impressed with your executive clout.

Many professional women feel that a plush, important-looking office is their most visible sign of power. Some even prefer a large office to salary increases because it is a visible sign of authority.

GOOD OFFICE ROLE MODELS

Most of the offices of the women I interviewed were attractive, comfortable, and quite egalitarian. Rather than feeling as if I were stumbling into some sort of James Bond subterfuge, I felt very much at home.

Many women informed me that they choose to have meetings following the tradition set by the Knights of the Round Table. With a round table, no one person can be at the head, or at the foot for that matter. A round table makes all concerned feel more at ease and on an equal footing.

Your office looks just like you. It is important to have an office that suits your personality. If your environment is totally out of sync with your mind and moods, you're likely to be equally out of sync with your job. Here are some tips designed to help you make your office homey to both you and your visitors:

Your office should be comfortable. You're going to be working there at least eight hours a day. Therefore, you don't want to sit in a chair that feels like something out of a medieval torture chamber. Think of what will make your visitors comfortable as well.

Keep efficiency in mind. Your office is not for aesthetic purposes only, so remember to furnish it with everything that is necessary for you to do a terrific job. Arrange the furniture in such a fashion that you don't need to roller-skate across the room every time you need to find a report.

Your office should reflect your personality. Just as your home makes a statement about who you are, so should your office. For example, Dr. Estelle Ramey is a chic, good-looking woman with a delightful sense of humor. Her office reflects her personality. Located in the middle of a stark, starchy hospital (Georgetown Medical School, where she is a professor), her office is an oasis of warmth and good taste. Amidst the strong wood paneling are delicate Japanese and Chinese objets d'art. On the lighter side, there is a picture of her husband inscribed "To my not-so-silent partner," and a needlepoint wall hanging that says, "I am my sister's keeper."

Keep it neat. You don't have to dust every two hours, but don't be a slob. Your office should always be neat and well organized.

Keep it uncluttered.

Extra clothes, makeup kit, extra shoes, and similar personal items should be carefully hidden. It's an excellent idea to have all of these things handy, just don't advertise the fact. People don't want to feel as if they have just walked into your closet.

THE IMPORTANCE OF OFFICE REDECORATION

When I had my own ad agency, my partners, typical artists, were more concerned about what went on paper than what went on their walls. They felt "we have no time to decorate." I totally disagreed, but fixed up my office after hours with my own money and my own furniture. I brought in a beautiful oriental rug from home, bought a classy-looking desk, and hung some Japanese prints on the wall. Before I knew it, everyone was congregating in my office because it was "so attractive." Clients were whisked into my showplace so they could be impressed with orderliness rather than having to wade through the piles of clutter in my partners' office. As a footnote, I later asked a client what made him decide to use our agency. He answered, "Well, when I saw your office and the care you put into it, I was hooked. I decided anyone who had such good taste should be designing my ads."

In a big corporation another fringe benefit is that a classy office will stand out from the rest. If all the other offices are blah blue and yours is a smashingly understated beige with elegant accessories, you will be remembered!

Finally, let me add that, whatever you buy for your office, make it of good quality. It's better to have blank walls than a tacky picture that looks like a paint-by-numbers design. Remember that a touch of class and good taste are the order of the day.

4
Power Failure

RECOGNIZING, ACQUIRING, AND USING POWER

Women are just discovering what men have known all along—that *power* can be fun. It's exciting, it's heady, it's sexy. We were told that Henry Kissinger, as secretary of state, was a sexy, sexy man. The most near-sighted viewer can tell that Dr. Kissinger is no dead ringer for Robert Redford. So it is obvious that his sex appeal has more to do with his role as a prime mover than his primeval good looks.

Power is what the whole women's movement was and still is about. We won the power to vote. Now we want the power to be considered equal under the law! Hence, the enormous power struggle over the ERA.

Power is essentially what this whole book is about. Women no longer are interested in having the doors opened for them. Today they want the doors opened to them. People, both male and female, must realize that women want the freedom in business that men have enjoyed for centuries. We want money, we want recognition, we want clout. In other words, we want *power*. As Gloria Steinem explains "Now, we are becoming the men we wanted to marry. Once women were trained to marry a doctor, not be one."[1]

Power remains a subtle, elusive thing. In this chapter I will discuss various definitions of power, why women in the past have been denied power, and some ways they can now get power. In addition, I have included profiles of some extremely powerful women to inspire you. So let's begin this potent subject of *womanpower* and find out how to get more power to you.

Power Failure: Reasons Why Women Fail

When addressing the question of why women fail, it is necessary to find out what we are doing wrong before we know how to remedy the problem. A beginning driver must learn the rules and meanings of safety signs before going out on the road. And likewise a beginning businesswoman must learn some rules, too.

THERE REALLY IS A GOOD-OLD-BOYS NETWORK AND, BELIEVE ME, YOU ARE DEFINITELY NOT ONE OF THE BOYS

I met my first good old boy when I was working for a movie company in Atlanta, Georgia, ten years ago. As director of publicity for the Southeast I traveled the area setting up movie promotions. Most of the men I dealt with had never seen a woman with a briefcase, but the majority, being Southern gentlemen, thought it was "cute" that a "little gal" like me had a man's job. One paunchy cigar-smoking man who looked like the prototype for the sheriff in *In the Heat of the Night* not only found my job presumptuous, but was annoyed that I had it. One night in Birmingham, Alabama, after a hectic movie opening, this man, a radio station owner, voiced his objections to my job.

"Look, little lady," he belched after too many Southern Comforts. "You're not bad at your job, but it's no job for a girl. There are too many men that could use that job and it ain't fair that you've got it."

I asked this man, who was looking more like a plantation owner at the time, if he himself wanted my job.

"No, but I know other men that do and they got families to s'port. Damn it, this is a man's world."

Let's face it, many men still see business as an all-male club and you, as a woman, are not going to be invited into its hallowed halls. Power, like the divine right of kings, has been a predominantly male prerogative for generations. Men aren't willingly going to hand over their crowns to women.

As Jane Trahey so aptly points out, "Why don't women move to the big power jobs? . . . because men have these jobs. Men want these jobs. Men love these jobs. They are exciting, profitable and powerful. What would ever make you think they want a woman to have them? Men are groomed for these jobs by men.

The big powers are handed down from generation to generation."[2]

Much of the good-old-boys network operates underground.
While everything seems totally fair and aboveboard at work, what
women don't realize is that many of the important business decisions are made during all-male tennis games, in the locker rooms,
at stag lunches, or during a seemingly innocuous viewing of a
Monday night football game.

Michael Korda in his best-selling book, *Power*, reports that
some businessmen are as devious as James Bond in their efforts
to keep women from becoming part of their exclusive club. He
explains that "Men will go to extraordinary lengths to invent power
structures that exist primarily to deprive successful women of
their autonomy."

In one tale of subterfuge, Korda warns businesswomen that, in
many companies, if it ever becomes necessary to add a woman to
an executive committee, the committee expands until it is too
big to serve any decision-making function. He further cautions
that "any job a woman does is downgraded the moment she has
proved she can do it."[3]

Korda's warnings on how men keep women from having power
sound dangerously like manuals on war games. However, I suppose if we were forced to think of business as the military, as
Betty Lehan Harragan insists we do, it is useful to know where
the hidden mine fields are.

I was hopeful with the new generation of businessmen and
-women that these power games would become relics of the past.
Unfortunately, younger women report that the old-boys network
is still very much a fact of life.

Valerie Slater, a young attorney, discusses her views on power
and the good-old-boys club. Slater's law firm, Steptoe and Johnson, is one of Washington's most prestigious, and its plush office
with a beautiful view of the city looks like the interior of an exclusive English men's club.

"Younger women have a different perspective on discrimination. There is very little sex discrimination in the educational
system. You are going to get your As if you do well on the test
because the education game is pretty much sex blind. After school,
scholarships and the whole bit, you expect to be treated equally.
You don't expect to run into any kind of problems. Nothing pre-

pared me for the kind of subtle differences that I detect here. My male colleagues are doing things that I just do not do. I'm not sent out to meet clients. It's that old-boys network. It just would not occur to them to have me do these things, because I'm a woman."

LEARNING NEW GAMES NEEDS TO BE PART OF YOUR GAME PLAN—WOMEN DON'T REALIZE THAT WORKING IS A GAME

The good old boys not only have a network; they also are well aware that working is a game and, in order to succeed, you have to know who the players are and which are the proper moves. To challenge these champions, I suggest you heed the advice of Betty Lehan Harragan. She says, essentially, that working is a game that women have begrudgingly been invited to play in, but have ever so conveniently not been given the rules. It seems comparable to being challenged by Boris Spassky to a game of chess, only to discover that he alone has access to the rules; worse yet, he changes them as he goes along.

Sometimes, just knowing that you are involved in a game rather than merely a business is half the battle. Harragan explains:

"Once you know the rules, it's easy to predict opponents' moves, at least easier than when you don't even know you're in a game where explicit rules govern the play."[4]

Marlene Sanders, correspondent at CBS News and three-time Emmy Award winner, attests to the fact that game playing and power politics are still very much part of the business arena.

Sanders, who was American Women in Radio and Television's 1975 Broadcast Woman of the Year, discusses this sporting subject with me.

"There are heavy politics in this business. You have to be on guard. I think a lot of women have a tendency to say, 'Well, I'll just do a good job and I'll be promoted and I'll get ahead.' They try to ignore cultivating the right people, and maneuvering around the way you have to do; unfortunately, you can't do one without the other. It's ridiculous to ignore that particular aspect. You have to do it."

WOMEN DON'T SEE THEMSELVES AS HAVING THE ABILITY TO
CONTROL THEIR OWN LIVES—THEY TURN THEIR DESTINIES
OVER TO MEN

We have all probably known a woman who we feel is so capa-
ble she could singlehandedly run General Motors, command an
entire army, revolutionize the stock market, and still have energy left over for writing a novel, while taking up jet-plane testing. To your bewilderment this person transforms before your
eyes one day when you ask her to make a simple decision. "Oh,
I couldn't make that kind of choice," she responds. "My husband
handles all of those things."

Estelle Ramey discusses this phenomenon. "The trouble with
women, as I see it, is that they may have an economic base and
therefore the power to control their lives, but they don't see
themselves as having that ability. So they throw away the power
that they really have. They give it away because they have been
taught to turn their destinies over to men. Therefore, having an
economic base doesn't give you the power to control your own
life unless you use the force that is inherent in it."

TO PARAPHRASE POGO, "I HAVE MET THE ENEMY AND HE IS
US"—SOMETIMES WOMEN'S WORST ENEMIES ARE WOMEN

Jeanne Lesem, the feisty, down-to-earth Family Page editor of
United Press International, has some strong views on why women
fail. As we sit in her comfortable New York apartment having
drinks, she discusses these.

"This whole business of women being their own worst enemies
is perfectly true. I think this is one of the biggest mistakes women
make. They are so busy fighting each other that they get a well-
deserved reputation for bitchiness, which is really applied to all
women rather than to those few who use this as their way to get
ahead. Since women are unsure of themselves to begin with, men
take advantage of that to set us at each other's throats."

Jo Foxworth embellishes this disturbing thought: "Women do
not trust themselves and therefore do not trust each other. Here
and there the walls of doubt are tumbling down, but the distrust
lingers.

"From sea to shining sea, I have asked female executives (present and future) to tell me what, in their opinion, is the biggest mistake women in business make. High on every list, and at the very top of many is: they don't help each other. Some put it a great deal more strongly. In Seattle one said: 'They stab you in the back!' In Dallas: 'They want to be the only woman around who has authority.' "[5]

Estelle Ramey has some fascinating thoughts on why women are aggressive to other women. "Women are as aggressive as hungry lions, but only towards other women. It is almost contrary to survival to be aggressive to men, but towards other women you can express aggression—like in bargain basements, competition for men, cattiness—all the things that are female aggression. This is always against women because you can get away with it. And men, of course, love it, they laugh at it. They call women catty—a term which trivializes female aggression. There is nothing that is more successful in keeping women in their place than seeing them as weak and ineffectual—like little girls, they're kind of cute, even when they get mad."

WOMEN SEE JOBS AS TEMPORARY AND THEY LACK SPECIFIC CAREER GOALS

More and more women today are planning long-range careers with specific ten-year plans, but in the past the majority of women worked only until they had children or until they earned enough money to pay off the first house mortgage. Unfortunately, conditioning dies hard, and the residual effects of this kind of short-term thinking are felt by many women today. Women in the past were so adaptable that they dutifully followed their husbands from place to place. They never questioned whether or not they had a choice. Today even the most dedicated career women sometimes have difficulty thinking of a job as something that they will do for their entire lives; they just weren't brought up that way.

Aileen Phillips, a public relations consultant, is a very successful woman, but she admits that her upbringing has caused her some problems.

"I was raised to be a hard worker, but I wasn't taught to see myself as a career woman. I didn't take advantage of a lot of golden career opportunities because I saw working as a fairly temporary thing. It was more important for me to have dates and lots of fun than prepare myself for a career."

Men have been conditioned to have "flight plans," whereas most women just keep circling the field, uncertain as to where they should land. Too many women amble along willy-nilly, taking whatever job comes along rather than purposefully planning where they will be in ten or fifteen years. Many women, looking back, see a career as fragmented as a broken stained-glass window. They think of their careers only intermittently. Their loyalties are divided among themselves, their husbands, and their children.

Jane Trahey discusses this pattern that keeps women's careers from soaring.

"Recently a women's college went on a search for a president. They wanted a woman. They thought it would be good PR. The search firm sent in the troops. Of the five really good prospects, there wasn't one who would give up her present security. Nor did the one from out of the city want to relocate. It would be too much of a hassle with husband and children. Sympathetically, she said, 'Oh, the kids are at that funny age—all their friends are in Cincinnati.' And smiling ruefully, she added, 'Besides, I don't think my husband would consider it. After all, his job is there.'

"Turn those tables around. Would a male administrator or professor turn down a chance at a presidency out of consideration for his wife's job and his children's school? You know that answer."[6]

More Power to You: How Women Can Get Clout

WE NEED AN OLD-BIDDY SYSTEM TO OFFSET THE OLD-BUDDY SYSTEM

We're all in this together, so we need to help each other. As Estelle Ramey pointed out to me, "No woman is an island." We need each other. Ramey, in her irreverent fashion, feels it is time to start the Old-Biddy System. "For years, when I needed a research assistant, I would call a friend in the sciences and say, 'Do you know a bright young person who would be interested?' and he sends me a bright young guy. We need a network now that sends bright young women."

The following story illustrates how former Carter aide Sarah Weddington, now director of the Washington-based Office of State-Federal Relations for Texas, put the good-old-girls network to use.

"When I was appointed to President Carter's staff, my job as general counsel in the Agriculture Department became available. At this time, a gentleman called me to say, 'I hear your job as general counsel is opening up. I have someone I want you to consider. His name is Robert _____.' I answered, 'OK, but we do have several women in mind.' He said, 'But you just had that job. I think those jobs ought to be rotated between men and women.' I answered, 'Fine, you've had it since 1887; now it's our turn.' "

Networking seems to be the key buzzword of the 1980s. However, for some women it was not a new thought. Gene Barnes explains, "Long before ERA came into existence, I was aware, and so were most of my friends, that there had to be a kind of unwritten alliance among women."

The only drawback to the network's being totally effective is that there are a few gaps in the net. Marlene Sanders talks about this problem:

"Right now we are not powerful or influential enough or visible enough in key jobs to be that helpful. The key jobs in broadcasting are held by men who tend to stick together, be it at lunch or playing tennis. That's where they will make decisions. It's very hard for women to get into that, and until women make up a big portion of that group, we're really not going to have it.

"The news business is still a boys' club and women are not members. Women still are not considered entirely equal. Even worse, women generally are not considered; we are outsiders. Unfortunately, the higher you go, the more discrimination you will face, and if you do air work, there will be discrimination in the kind of assignments you'll get."

Beverly Lannquist fortunately sees this whole situation changing for the better.

"I think that the old-girls network is just starting to develop. It takes a while. You need to have the experience and to have been around. There weren't that many women in important positions twenty years ago.

"But this is changing now that there are an enormous number of women in the pipeline who are achieving good positions. I'm in my thirties and I figure I'm in the group that's in the leading edge. There are a lot of women in their early thirties who are coming along and behind us is a rapidly growing group that is achieving good positions. I think that in ten or fifteen years there will be many women, whom I know personally, who will be in top positions around the country. And that's only going to increase as time goes by."

I AM MY SISTER'S KEEPER

For some time women have been flattered by men who tell them that "they think like a man" and that they seem a cut above most women. I remember when Charles, a business partner in my advertising agency, complimented me on my work performance by saying, "I've never worked with any woman like you. You don't cry or fall apart when the going gets tough." His ultimate compliment was, "You're almost my equal." But he added, "You're different from most women. Most of them are impossible to work with."

Reflecting on this praise, I realized that, rather than being thrilled that I was singled out as exceptional, I was annoyed that he thought so poorly of my sisters. Being the only perfect female in the world is, after all, a heavy burden.

Estelle Ramey has the following thought for women: "Women have to be prepared to recognize one very important thing: As long as women as a group are seen as inadequate compared with men, then every single woman, no matter how successful, is tarred with that brush. You can't separate yourself from your own kind. No woman is going to be seen as anything other than a woman. She's not going to be seen as one of the boys because she's not one of the boys. You can't get women into the roles they should play by telling them they're different, or that they are slobs intellectually, or weak and ineffectual. As long as that idea exists as a general concept, all women are going to be viewed as somewhat less desirable in the pilot's seat."

Gloria Steinem concurs with Ramey and adds: "Even if we [women] achieve a little success in the world and think of ourselves as 'different,' we don't want to associate with our group. . . . We want to be the only woman in the office, or the only black family on the block, or the only Jew in the club."[7]

PEOPLE TO PEOPLE—MEN AND WOMEN NEED TO
HELP EACH OTHER

Sarah Caldwell, the guiding light for the Boston Opera, put
things into perspective when I asked her how women could help
other women. She laughed and then replied, after some thought,
"The best way is not for women only helping other women, but
for people helping people. In my profession, music making helps
both men and women."

Dr. Ramey had some pertinent thoughts on this subject. "One
must never forget that there have always been men who are very
supportive, and you have to make use of them, too. You have to
bring them into the system. You need to have men on your side.
Remember, men had to vote to give women the vote. Also, more
men in this country, percentage-wise, are more in favor of ERA
than women."

IF YOU WANT TO BE A MEMBER OF THE CLUB, YOU HAVE TO
LEARN TO PAY YOUR DUES

Some women are looking for magic formulas for success; unfortunately, no such formula exists. Amy Greene has some strong
opinions on this subject:

"Nobody wants to pay her dues. Everybody wants to be Sammy
Davis, not knowing that he's been singing and dancing since he
was eighteen months old. *There is no such thing* as an overnight
success."

Dame Fortune has little to do with most American success stories. Hard work seems to be one of the main ingredients for success. Amy Greene, addressing this topic, says, "As corny and
trite as it sounds, there is no easy way to success, there is no
short route to the top. You've just got to work your ass off. It's
that simple. And in a totally male-oriented business world, we,
unfortunately, have to work twice as hard as men."

MAKE CERTAIN YOU ARE NOT IN THE LINE OF FIRE—KNOW
THE DIFFERENCE BETWEEN LINE AND STAFF JOBS

While you are working hard, make certain you are working in
the right direction. Too many women naively think that pure,

unrestrained hard work is the secret of success. Unfortunately, this type of virtue isn't always rewarded in the business world. To get to the top you have to understand your company's power route, then determine if you are on the right road or going up a blind alley. As Betty Lehan Harragan explains, "Women are rarely guided in the right direction, primarily because the 'natives'—predominately male—don't really want us to get there. When we are promoted under pressure of equal employment laws, we are usually pushed straight ahead in a narrow specialty field—a route that ultimately leads to a dead end or sidetrack."

To be able to zoom along the highway of success one must know the difference between line jobs and staff jobs. According to Harragan, "Line jobs have a direct connection with a company's profits; 'staff' jobs do not. Theoretically, the function of the chief executive officer is to oversee the organization and to insure the profitable contributions of each part. Those which turn out to be nonproductive or overly expensive are eventually cut back or dispensed with. All the talent and hard work in the world won't get you ahead if your efforts are devoted to a task viewed as nonessential by the senior officers."[8]

MONEY TALKS—"TO HAVE POWER, WOMEN FIRST
HAVE TO HAVE SOME ECONOMIC CLOUT"

It's one thing to pay your dues, but it takes money to buy the club. Money may not be the only ingredient for power, but it certainly is impossible to have any real control without it. As Dr. Ramey says, "To have power, women first have to have some economic clout."

Money is the key to equality, according to Ramey. "Women must learn to give money. Women have always been prepared to impoverish themselves to buy new dresses to make themselves look attractive. They must learn that if they really want to look attractive, they will have to change the total image of women."

Dr. Ramey is the type of woman who practices what she preaches. She gives the money that she makes on the "hot lecture circuit" to support homes for battered wives and to set up scholarships to train women in the sciences. At Georgetown University, Ramey has set up the Association for Women in Science Education and has helped finance it with her own funds.

TAKE YOURSELF SERIOUSLY AND
DON'T GIVE AWAY FREE ADVICE

Recently, an owner of a successful department store called me and suggested that he "wanted to pick my brains" regarding his new advertising campaign. He felt that this brain-picking—a term I find singularly unappetizing—should take place over drinks. My response to this invitation was: "I charge one hundred dollars an hour for advertising consultation; why don't we set up an appointment for 10 A.M. Thursday?"

By answering in this manner, I made it very clear that my brains were not free pickings and that I was not going to give him the benefit of my ten years' experience in exchange for a poorly made margarita.

Women are often so flattered that someone is seeking their advice that they are delighted to give away information they should be selling. When I owned my advertising agency, I received incessant phone calls from people who wanted me to think up cute slogans for their favorite charity or political campaign. The usual ploy was that since writing headlines is such fun, I shouldn't mind doing one for an acquaintance—gratis, of course. My response was, "You're right, I do think coming up with good headlines is a lot of fun; it's also profitable for me and the way I make my living. I would be delighted to help you. I charge one hundred dollars an hour."

If this tactic didn't work, I had one more line that usually stopped them in their tracks. When they were pointing out that, since it was so much fun to be a writer, I should produce something for the pure joy of it, I answered back: "Well, I assume your doctor and lawyer love their jobs, too. But they still have to make a living since it's hard to buy groceries on pure love. My lawyer, who takes enormous pleasure in his work, charges one hundred dollars an hour."

Amy Greene puts a high premium on her time and certainly doesn't give away free advice.

"When a man pays you a certain amount of money, he'll listen to you. I never go to lunch. People call up and say, 'Let me pick your brains, I'll take you to lunch.' I answer, 'I don't want to go to lunch today. I'll meet you somewhere, we'll talk for a while and I'll send you a bill.' Right away, everything changes."

Greene continues, "I will not discuss a total color scheme with a major advertiser for nothing and certainly not for a piece of veal and a salad. But many women will give away what they know because of their own insecurities—they don't feel they are worth a hundred dollars an hour."

OF COURSE YOU CAN, OF COURSE YOU CAN—BE A RISK TAKER

Women for generations have risked childbirth, assumed the responsibility for their children's lives, and in general put themselves on the line over and over again. Unfortunately, many women aren't able to translate this risk-taking ability into climbing the corporate ladder. Instead, they worry incessantly about the consequences of falling off. Risk taking is part of the challenge of any business and can have its positive aspects. Probably you were protected and secure in your nest of home and hearth, but hasn't it always been more fun to try your wings and soar? So what if you fell a few times on the way. We all fall in every phase of our lives. And remember, men haven't been 100 percent risk-free in the business world. Every successful man has taken risks and fallen on his respective face a few times. In this respect equality cuts both ways.

DON'T BE AFRAID OF SUCCESS—IT'S MUCH MORE FUN THAN FAILURE

For many women, failure seems much more comfortable than success. Women are taught from birth to cope with failure, but very few have been taught to deal with success. I see this unfortunate phenomenon changing, since all the influential women profiled here seemed very comfortable and happy with their success.

THE SKY'S THE LIMIT—RAISE YOUR EXPECTATION LEVEL

Women have to stop thinking, "This is a good job for a woman; I'd better not risk job security by trying for a higher one." If Orville and Wilbur and Amelia Earhart had felt that way, we'd all be grounded today.

BELIEVE IN YOURSELF, AND, BELIEVE ME, EVERYONE ELSE
WILL, TOO—CONFIDENCE IS CONTAGIOUS

Years ago, when I was working as director of publicity for the
movie company in Atlanta, I was ordered by my boss in Hollywood to put on a world premiere for one of the movies I was
working on. The closest I had ever come to a world premiere up
until that time was watching one on the Rona Barrett show. I
wasn't about to let my boss in on that little fact, however, so I
calmly told him I would arrange the whole thing. Then I called
up a friend in the movie business and asked him, "How do you
put on a world premiere? He gave me a blow-by-blow descrip-
tion and helped me pull the whole thing off.

This bold kind of response was one I had learned from the men
I had worked with. I observed that whereas many women (and
some men, also) would panic and confess that they didn't have
the remotest idea how to do such-and-such, many men would
confidently accept an assignment and then call up a knowledge-
able colleague and ask for help.

So, take a tip from your male counterparts. Don't stupidly say,
"I couldn't do that." Get your good-old-girls (or boys) network
going and call someone to find out how to do whatever you need
to do. It does wonders for your confidence.

BE WILLING TO LEARN

You can never know too much about your job. You can learn
from everybody around you; just keep your eyes and ears open.
As Amy Greene suggests, "Women must be sponges at work and
absorb everything they can."

Marie Hirst, the first woman executive at Sperry & Hutchin-
son and the president of The Hirst Company, an Albuquerque
public relations firm, puts it thus: "Sometimes women talk too
much and don't listen and don't pick up on what is going on around
them. I know I used to do that until I observed my husband. At
meetings he was like a clam, but he took in all the information
that was being given out. Then, when he spoke, he said something really intelligent, using all the information he had gath-
ered. It's a good tip for women to follow."

NEVER UNDERESTIMATE THE POWER OF A WOMAN

What, then, can we now conclude about power? We have learned (if we didn't already know it) that women have the ability and opportunity to attain power. We certainly have the burning desire for more clout. We realize that not only do we deserve it, but also that power can be enormously challenging and fun.

That is not to say that power will fall into your lap. It won't. Happy-ever-after endings occur only in fairy tales and old Horatio Alger novels. These are times that try women's souls—and build women's vision. We must become that much stronger and more resilient until we get what we want. Furthermore, we must stay united, for in unity there is strength.

Never underestimate the power of any collective force, nor the weakness of a house divided. Today is not the time to fight and to compete. Let us take a page from the book of grass-roots organizations that have accomplished mighty deeds. The Women's Movement, the Peace Movement, the Environmental Movement were each sustained by a small, united group who had strong wants and ideals. Power in the workplace is an attainable goal for working women—and for you. If we all pull together, never again will anyone ever underestimate the power of a woman.

"But standing alone we learned our power; we repudiated man's counsels forevermore; and solemnly vowed that there should never be another season of silence until we had the same rights everywhere on this green earth, as man." *Elizabeth Cady Stanton*

PROFILES OF POWERFUL WOMEN

"The sudden acquisition of power by those who have never had it
before can be intoxicating. . . ."   *Toni Carabillo*

To find out who possesses this elusive element called power
and how it is obtained, I went straight to the source's mouth and
interviewed some of the most powerful women in the country.
They all had one characteristic in common. Each exuded self-
confidence and had a very definite sense of who she was and
where she was going.

The four profiles in this chapter have been chosen out of many
interviews to illustrate for you what powerful women think about
power, like about power, have learned about power. In these
quick profiles, you will gain many insights into power, all grounded
in personal experiences and valuable for you to consider as you
come to grips with power as women's natural right.

PROFILE
Estelle Ramey, Scientist

If I had to pick only one woman to serve as a role model for
women seeking power, I would choose Dr. Estelle Ramey. She
wears the cloak of power as comfortably as most women wear a
flattering new dress. A professor of physiology and biophysics at
Georgetown University and a renowned specialist in endocrine
research, she is one of the leading scientists in the field. She is
presently researching the sex differences in longevity.

Dr. Ramey was named one of the "100 Most Important Women
in America" by *The Ladies Home Journal*, October 1983. The list
of her credentials and research output are almost as long as this
entire book and her ventures into the popular press include articles in *Harper's*, *Ms.* magazine, and many of the major women's
magazines.

She is, as she puts it, "a hot item on the feminist lecture circuit," and after meeting her, I could certainly understand why.
In my opinion, she is the strongest and most refreshing voice of
feminism speaking in the country today. She combines the wit of
a stand-up comic with the wisdom of Eleanor Roosevelt.

She is a series of delightful paradoxes. Her appearance is what one would have described in preliberation terms as "ladylike." Ramey quickly informs me, however, that she doesn't even know what a lady is, "but I doubt that I'm one—I'm more of a peasant." The incongruity continues as she answers my myriad questions. Her decidedly erudite professional tone is nicely seasoned with salty sailor's language.

One of the first things Dr. Ramey tells me is how she donates the money from her whirlwind lecture tours to what she considers appropriate causes: homes for battered wives and scholarships for women medical students. She explains that "having been a poor girl it's very nice in my declining years to become a lady bountiful."

As hard as I try to be respectful, the term "declining years" makes me smile. If the Roman Empire had been in a "decline" similar to Estelle Ramey's, we would all be speaking Latin today. Although Dr. Ramey was born in 1917, "just as women were tooling up for the right to vote," she is anything but declining.

In her articulate fashion, Dr. Ramey gives me a simple, yet incisive response. "The ultimate power is the ability to control your own destiny. That means you have to be beyond the control of other people. Power to me is essentially the ability to control one's life, basically in economic terms; I'm convinced that the control of the economic base of a life is the sine qua non of control of every other aspect of a life. If you have no economic base, you are a hostage to society."

Pausing for a moment to chat amiably with the cleaning woman, Dr. Ramey once again addresses the question of power.

"That old aphorism—that money doesn't buy everything—is perfectly true. It sure as hell doesn't buy poverty. Poverty doesn't buy dignity nor does it buy love. There is more mental illness in this country and in any country among the poor than among the rich. Getting back to the definition of power, I believe that power ultimately resides in an economic base."

Is Ramey going to slow down in her "declining years"? Not a chance. As she explains in her irreverent fashion: "In three years I'll be seventy years old and I am depending on my heritage from good peasant stock to continue to bedevil the establishment until women are recognized as the biologic marvels they really are. Age will not wither my capacity to make life a misery for those

who put roadblocks in the path of achieving human dignity for all
of us with ovaries."

PROFILE
Cathleen Black, Publisher

Cathleen Black has power and plenty of it. As president of *USA
Today*, she is, at thirty-nine one of the new breed of women who
are moving into top managerial positions.

The attractive no-nonsense blonde admits that she has a great
deal of clout. She defines power as "having the responsibility and
the authority to make things happen."

However, she adds in her staccato clip that power is often overrated. "People seem to get hung up on the power trip. What
do most people mean by power anyway? Is power getting on a
corporate jet? If so, that's fun. I like it; I did it yesterday. Is it
having a staff say 'Good morning' with a different kind of respect
because you have a new title and a new job? I think all these kind
of things are really the trivial part of it. I tend not to think about
this superficial part a lot.

"I think what is more important than the trappings of power is
achieving goals. You need to say this is my goal and that's what I
want to achieve and do it or not do it."

Black is clearly achieving her goals. Prior to joing *USA Today*,
she was publisher of *New York* magazine and in that role was the
first woman ever to be publisher of a weekly consumer magazine.
She was also a type of "miracle worker" in reviving *New York*,
which had been floundering and at the lowest financial ebb in its
ten-year history.

How did she accomplish this? "We doubled the ad pages because, quite simply, I am a terrific salesperson, and I have good
judgment. I can sense how to put the spokes back in a wheel."

No doubt Black learned her sound basic training from her years
as associate publisher of *Ms.* magazine. "We were not only selling a page of advertising, but we were selling a changing woman's
market and really convincing them that women were thinking
differently about their lives."

Black has certainly not forgotten the women's movement at
USA Today. As she explains, "In *USA Today*, almost every single
day there is a picture of a woman in either the news or business

section who has received some kind of promotion, recommendation or recognition. I think that this is a subtle way to remind people that this is happening constantly. We just show one picture, but it is representative of all the people around the country who got promoted, got a new title or a new job."

Black is enthusiastic about the new influence of working women and sees a bright future for the upcoming generation. She thinks that women's lives are irreversibly changed by the women's movement or, as she puts it, "Once you come off the farm, you're never going to go back again. This is what has happened to women in the work world. Most women have discovered that work is exciting, demanding, and the money is very important. For many women, the idea that they can make a lot of money is a real thrill. Women want to have their own sense of fulfillment and satisfaction that is not just being a parent and a wife. I don't think once that clock has been turned forward that we will go back on that at all."

Black feels the key word for women in the eighties is "options." "In the seventies, the first real decade of the women's movement, women's blinders were opened and our vision expanded to have a much greater dream. We talked a great deal about how options and alternatives for women had to be there. Today most of us would agree that the options are there and that we can do really whatever we want to do. Now that we have achieved that, I think some women will say, 'What I really want to do is to stay home for a few years with my small children.' And they will do that. Then they will figure out a way to check back into the work force."

Cathleen Black's options are a remarriage and no children. She "doesn't find it so hard to juggle a marriage" and for two years, in the best spirit of the eighties, she and her husband, Thomas W. Harvey, general counsel to the U.S. Information Agency, were a commuting couple. "My husband lived in Washington and I lived in New York and we got together on weekends. Now my base of operations is in Washington, so we're really in the same city although I am gone probably somewhere between three and four days a week. So I really don't see him any more than I did before. In many ways, less, because the time commitments on this particular job right now are enormous. I think it would be a lot harder if you have small children."

Black hadn't been too optimistic about changes in the American family until she recently gave a speech to teenage presidential interns from all around the country. "I said that I thought that one of the biggest problems for working women was it meant they really had three full-time jobs—children, home and their jobs. I told them that I had recently read an article that said that the average male was now spending fourteen hours a week on things around the house. I admitted that I found it hard to believe that men spent that much time and the group booed me. So I challenged them. I said 'I'll bet your fathers don't spend fourteen hours a week doing things around the home.' Half of them put their hands up and said, 'Yes, they did.'

"I was delighted and shocked at the same time. Things definitely are getting better for women."

Cathleen Black and *USA Today* may be two of those things that are helping women's lives to improve.

PROFILE
Jo Foxworth, Advertising Executive

Jo Foxworth combines Southern gentility, Yankee ingenuity, and Midwestern friendliness. When we chatted on the telephone, I felt as if I were calling a friend from my home state of Indiana. She and I had never met, and yet I felt I had known her for years.

From her low-key manner, one would never guess, on first encounter, that Foxworth is one of the most important women in the advertising industry. Among other things, she is owner of a successful New York advertising agency, has been named Advertising Woman of the Year by five professional organizations, wrote a column for eleven years for *Advertising Age*, and is a public speaker in great demand. She is the author of two guidebooks for businesswomen, *Boss Lady* and *Wising Up*.

Though advertising is now a labor of love, she got into it for the money. "When you are born poor in Mississippi, you think a lot about financial security. When I started out, the money was in advertising and I was under pressure to make some money."

Foxworth fulfilled her childhood goal and is indeed making lots of lucre, but she is one of those fortunate people for whom working is fun. "Every now and then I think of getting out of the ad business, but I'm like the old firehorse. Advertising is so much a part of me. I really love it. I love creating concepts and writing copy."

Like many successful executives, Foxworth works "all the time. I seem to feel like I'm stealing if I'm not working. You see my work is fun for me. That's how I get my jollies. For instance, the other morning I woke up early and decided I needed to write the speech I was going to make to the Cosmetic Executive Women. I got up and looked in the mirror and decided I looked like that old woman they brought out of Shangri-La. If you remember, in the movie, Ronald Colman brought her out on his back; she was a gorgeous young thing, and he rounded a bend on this mountain pass and the cold air hit her and it all went. So that gave me the idea of the speech and I simply got a yellow pad and a pen and got back into bed, wrote the speech and had the time of my life."

Foxworth hasn't always loved all her jobs, however. "I have had a few jobs that were drags, but the one I had in Louisville was the most difficult. I hated my boss—he was a man that kept his desk on a platform. When he finally fired me, I was relieved because when a big man thinks small, all you can do is run."

Foxworth kept her delightful sense of humor during this ordeal. "He fired me when I corrected his pronunciation. He called me a prima donna. I quickly retorted, 'The word is *preeeema-donna!*' You see, I don't like being called names ever, particularly by people who can't pronounce them."

After working for many more people, both good and bad, Foxworth decided to become her own "boss lady." She thinks that starting one's own business is "almost the only solution for getting power. A few women do make it to the higher level of corporations, but not many, and certainly none in the executive suite. Women simply do not get into shot-calling jobs, unless they own the company."

Which naturally brings the conversation to the subject of power. Foxworth defines power "as the ability to say yes or no and make it stick about anything that has to do with the company. Like whether we are going to expand, move closer to town, redecorate, pay more rent or whether to hire ten people or ten thousand—you know the decisions that really count."

Foxworth thinks that advertising is a good field for women and has the following advice for aspiring advertising recruits: "Get in at any salary you can and work your head off. Make yourself indispensable to the person you're reporting to. Let management know at the very beginning that you expect to do a very good job for the company and by the same token, you expect the company to do a lot for you. That's not asking too much."

Although the Mississippi native is a staunch feminist and is very helpful to other women, she has definite ideas on the politics of hiring women. "What I will not do is to give a particular break to anybody on account of gender. I think there is only one reason to hire someone and that is if they are very good."

She is good at answering the newest version of that inevitable question, "What do women want?" "I think that men are getting more and more used to us although I still hear a lot of men say 'I don't know how to treat you girls anymore. I don't know whether to open the doors for you or what.' " With her usual candor, Foxworth replies, "Why don't you treat us like you treat each other?"

Foxworth treats young women with respect and is a role model to many. After traveling around the country giving speeches to the next generation, she is optimistic about the future of women in business. However, she thinks some of the new breed of women have certain limitations. "I think women do not set their sights high enough. They do not let management know what they want and what they are willing to do in order to get it."

"Many women haven't set their goals and seem unsure of themselves. They don't seem to know who they are. What I tell them in commencement addresses and workshops is 'Unless you know who you are and what you want to do, somebody else will decide for you.' "

When asked why she thought younger women were sometimes confused about their goals, Foxworth replied: "There are too many choices. It's much easier if the choices are vanilla, chocolate and strawberry. Now there are twenty-seven flavors. It used to be that all women could do was teach school or clerk in a store. Now the world has opened up to them."

Knowing what her future holds in store has never been a problem for Foxworth. "I just want to keep doing what I am doing. I am very interested in all areas of communications, and right now I am working on a film with a very brilliant and gifted woman who was in the theatre and a film producer. I don't know whether we will get it off the ground or not. Every time you get a movie produced either in Hollywood or on television, another star has risen in the East."

If Foxworth pulls this off in her usual style, watch for that star in the East.

PROFILE
Gene Barnes, Public Relations Specialist

Although she is an influential and respected member of the public relations/marketing community, Gene Barnes, president of Barnes Associates, a public relations and marketing agency, has never let power go to her head. She is modest, soft-spoken, has a nice dry sense of humor and keeps herself in perspective. She is also a champion of women's rights and networking. No matter how busy she is (and she is a confessed workaholic), she always has time to help a colleague.

She has definite opinions on what power should and should not be. "What I do is work toward the possibility of giving the people for whom I work recognition and notoriety and a position or prestige so that they in turn have power. And that satisfies me. I think when you contribute to someone's knowledge, entertainment or enjoyment, you are wielding a kind of power by virtue of how much you contribute. I don't think of it as sitting up on a pinnacle and playing with people's lives like marionettes on strings. That would not be in keeping with my way of living or doing business."

Barnes does wield tremendous behind-the-scenes power. She has had direct impact on the careers of her clients, including Ann-Margret, Julie Andrews, Lucille Ball, Jimmy Stewart, Captain Kangaroo, Ringling Brothers Circus, Exxon, Revlon, The Emily Post Institute, the New York Chapter of the National Academy of Television Arts and Sciences, and Pfizer, Inc.

As she sits surrounded by pictures of the stars and the products she represents, Barnes reflects on how women are being affected by power today. "Power seems to be the buzzword of the eighties. There seem to be so many books and seminars dedicated to power. I suppose it is because the whole world has suddenly opened up to women and they're instinctively attracted to the modus operandi that men have grown up with all their lives. In other words, women are learning to play the game now that men have always played."

She has the following tips on how women can acquire power and in general move up in their career paths. "I think the most important thing is to learn to be objective. You have to be able to step back from a situation and go off by yourself and just figure out the pros and cons and the rights and wrongs of the situation and try to keep emotion and personal feelings out of it and just look at the situation as it is.

"And you have to use a great deal of diplomacy and patience along with objectivity not to ever lose sight of what you want to do."

Barnes attributes her success to having carefully formulated goals. She feels that objectives are essential to obtaining power.

"Women have to be willing to size up a situation and redirect their goals if that's what's required. In other words, they have to approach it from the same point of view that a man would. If there's some kind of goal that you want to accomplish, look at the successful men in your office. They would never waste their time trying to accomplish the impossible. So you need to go around, above, or underneath, or join forces with someone else and go in another direction and try to attack it from that point of view. In other words, use another channel.

"Women have to learn to be more flexible. You can't be rigid in your approach in any way. You have to learn how to fence. You have to parry, thrust and then step back and wait for the next opportunity to make your point."

Barnes, a pragmatic optimist, is encouraged about the future of businesswomen and in particular, the dual-career family. (She has been part of a two-paycheck marriage for twenty-six years and her husband, Wade, is chairman of the board of Barnes Associates.)

"I've been doing the publicity for a woman traveling around the country for American Home Foods and we're seeing some interesting new trends. Men, it seems, are gradually getting used to the idea of having to assume part of the responsibility of not only the household, but the children. Dual-career families are making their influence felt in the business community. Manufacturers of food products are focusing their attention on men and children since many of them are now doing most of the shopping."

5

Sex Fifth Avenue:
A Deportment Story

SEX AND SEXISM AT THE OFFICE

"There is a supposed compliment that goes like this: 'Gee, you're really good. You think like a man.' When somebody says it to Gladys Spellman, she says, 'Yeah, I know, I'm having an off day, I'll be myself tomorrow.' "
Eileen Shanahan
VIEWS FROM WOMEN ACHIEVERS

Although militant feminists may take issue with me, I still believe Freud was right about some things. Just because he didn't know what women wanted doesn't mean he was all bad. After all, we weren't so sure what we wanted either. For instance, I continue to agree with the venerable Viennese gentleman's theory that sex is the underlying factor in most aspects of our life. We are not, nor should we want to be, sexless creatures. Sex has stood the test of time and is here—thank goodness—to stay. Not only is sex a fact of life in our personal sphere, but it plays a significant role in our business life as well. It can, in fact, indeed be a pleasant part of our working life.

Dr. Estelle Ramey points out that working in a nunnery probably wouldn't be that much fun. She reasons, "Sexual tension between men and women is pleasant. It makes for a fuller life. Excluding one sex entirely from your business life would be like excluding one sex entirely from your social life. There would be a deficit. You could have a good party but it would be a different party. You would be missing something."

Of late we women have learned about this new style of freer sensuality—and about everything else we ever wanted to know about sex. One of the main insights to be gleaned from the recent glut of sex books is that women are every bit as sexual as men. We have learned to be comfortable with our sexuality and have discovered it is yet another way in which we are equal to the male of the species.

While we enjoy being sexually liberated, however, we don't relish being treated as sex objects, especially in the business world. Letty Cottin Pogrebin in her book, *Getting Yours*, puts this very real problem into focus by explaining, "What we rightfully resent and recoil at is the attitude that views us as objects for male sexual fantasies, as automatic partners in daytime peccadillos or as porno diversions at a dull sales conference. This attitude both dehumanizes women and costs us money."[1]

In other words, pleasurable sexual tension is acceptable and even enjoyable behavior, but when the harmless sensuality turns to abusive sexual harassment, the situation changes drastically. We, as businesswomen, therefore need to know how to deal with all aspects of sex in the working world because, as Jane Trahey so aptly puts it, "Unless you're going to work for the Trappists, sex is going to have its place."[2] Our responsibility as mature businesswomen is keeping sex in its proper place. We obviously will not tolerate being treated as sex objects, but neither do we want to feel that we have to go to work dressed in protective armor. The correct approach obviously lies somewhere in between.

THIS IS NOT THE MASTERS AND JOHNSON HOUR, THE HITE OF SEXUALITY OR KINSEY REPORTS TO THE NATION—WHAT, THEN, CAN YOU EXPECT FROM THIS CHAPTER?

When I was doing research on this subject, a curious thing happened. My friends assumed I was conducting some sort of sex clinic in my backyard—people I hadn't seen since kindergarten started calling to ask if I needed any more consenting adults for my study. Never have I felt more popular and never have people been more misinformed. Whereas this book might sell thousands more copies if it were entitled *The Joy of Business Sex*, and whereas conducting on-the-spot research might have been a lot more fun, I am afraid I must inform you that this chapter will not teach you one more kinky thing you might want to know about sex.

What I will discuss in this chapter is, first, how to handle various sexual harassment situations at work. There will be tips on how to turn down advances without turning down your opportunity to advance. The types of harassment discussed will run the gamut from the mild—albeit annoying—situation of being called "sweetheart" by your co-workers to the extremely serious problem of a man's insisting that if you don't sleep with him you will lose your job.

Harassment is one thing, but what if *you* are the one who is interested in someone in your office? Is it appropriate to have an affair with someone you work with? Do you know the consequences? Are they worth it? Some people are even encouraging office romances as the new chic trend. The issue of office romances is quite a controversial subject. Today is a tricky time to be a businesswoman because the rules about sex in the office are changing as fast as today's headlines. So what's a woman to do? How do you handle the situation if the affair turns into something quite serious? Or what about the women who sexually harass their male subordinates—is this what we mean by equality?

How about travel rules on sex? What do you do when the office Clark Kent turns into Super Lech before your very eyes? What if you want to have a harmless fling? Will it damage your career? Do you view business travel as a good way to meet men or are you looking for tips on how not to get picked up? All these sexual subjects and more will be covered in this chapter. So without further ado, let's get on with this deportment story.

THERE ARE ALAS, DEAR READER, NO SIMPLE SOLUTIONS

Had it not been for a total lack of aptitude and talent, I would have chosen to be a chemist rather than a writer—for the simple reason that I love formulas. I like knowing that, if x happens, all I have to do is apply y and the situation will remedy itself. However, although we seem to be a generation of people seeking simple answers, we don't often find them. For handling sexual harassment at the office, no one magic formula exists that will work for all women in all situations. What works beautifully for me might be a disaster for you and vice versa.

How you deal with any of the following problems will depend on your personality, your conditioning, your age, and your individual style. I find humor usually works well for me, but you might prefer the straightforward approach. So, as in most aspects of life, you have to be yourself and deal with these situations in the manner you find most comfortable. Where it is appropriate, I will discuss various approaches that correspond with different types of personality.

One other factor to consider in this complicated affair is what type of man you are dealing with. There is quite a difference in the way you should handle a Good Old Boy who thinks you should be home raising children and azaleas, compared with an enlightened man of good will who wants nothing more than to treat you in an unchauvinistic way. Human chemistry is, as I noted, a lot more complicated than what takes place in the lab.

If Sex is the Question, What is the Answer? Various Ways of Handling Different Types of Sexual Harassment Problems

What is sexual harassment, anyway?   Before we start discussing how best to deal with problems of sexual harassment, it might be useful to first define what is meant by the term. On November 10, 1980, the Equal Employment Opportunity Commission published final guidelines that affirmed its long-held position that sexual harassment in the workplace is a violation of Title VII of the 1964 Civil Rights Act.

The EEOC defines harassment on the basis of sex in its new guidelines as: "Unwelcomed sexual advances, requests for sexual favors and other verbal or physical conduct of a sexual nature when submission to such conduct is made either explicitly or implicitly a term or condition of an individual's employment; submission to or rejection of such conduct by an individual is used as the basis for employment decisions affecting the individual; or such conduct has the purpose or effect of unreasonably interfering with an individual's work performance or creating an intimidating, hostile or offensive working environment."

According to Muffet Foy Cuddy, Equal Opportunity Programs bureau chief with the New Mexico State Highway Department, "This definition deals with sexual harassment in such subtle forms as leering, verbal and visual harassment. It is much broader and a more difficult concept to deal with than sexual harassment in its most blatant forms."

How serious a problem is sexual harassment—what are the

chances that it could happen to me?   Unhappily, sexual harassment is an enormous problem today, and the chances are very
high that you will be sexually harassed at some point in your
working career. As a matter of fact, sexual harassment of working
women has reached epidemic proportions in this country. ABC
News examined this problem and reported the following alarming facts: ". . . most of the 42 million women in the U.S. work
force have been subjected to some form of sexual harassment,
whether it's a comment, a pinch, or an outright proposition. . . .
About 90 percent of the women on the average are saying that
sexual harassment is a serious job problem. About 70 percent
report that they have experienced it personally one or more times.
This is the scary part: 52 percent are reporting that sometime in
their working lives they have either quit or been fired because of
this type of sexual abuse on the job."

*If it's that serious, how come women don't talk about it
more?*   Women, who have been raised to be passive, often feel
as if everything that happens to them is their own fault. Sexual
harassment is no exception. Women, therefore, have often suf-
fered sexual harassment in silence, assuming that nothing could
be done, that it was their personal dilemma, that they were
somehow at fault for not being able to avoid it, or even that it was
somehow an inevitable part of women's lives.

THE WHO, WHAT, WHERE, AND WHY OF SEXUAL
HARASSMENT—BASICALLY POWER IS THE NAME OF THE GAME

Like rape, sexual harassment often has very little to do with
sexual attraction. Instead, it is another type of power play that
men use against women. Dr. Ramey explains: "The women who
are sexually harassed are the vulnerable women; it has nothing
to do with beauty, age, or anything else. You can be eighty years
old and there are guys who are going to see you as vulnerable
and use this as a power play against you. They'll dominate you,
especially if you're economically defenseless and you're afraid of
losing your job."

The woman Ramey is describing is most likely to be a secretary
or clerical worker, who is probably poorly paid to begin with,
can't afford to quit her job, and generally doesn't have the re-
sources to pursue costly harassment court cases.

THIS IS NO TIME TO BE SMUG, EXECUTIVE WOMEN—YOU'RE
ALSO A PRIME TARGET FOR HARASSMENT

Middle-management women do not escape the clutches of sexual harassment either. It may seem like a contradiction, but in
fact corporate men are interested in harassing executive women
for the same reason they are in bothering lower-level women:
power. Some men want to take an important woman down a few
notches, back to where she belongs. What better way to do it
than by sexually harassing her? It's the same tactic such men use
on secretaries.

*Well, at least if you are a professional woman and get har-
assed, you can fight back, can't you? The consequences aren't as
dastardly, are they?*   Most professional women who quit or are
fired from jobs because of sexual harassment aren't likely to go
directly on welfare. However, their careers are frequently dam-
aged. In addition, the emotional and psychological price that
professional women pay for this type of abuse is very high. Lin
Farley in *Sexual Shakedown* discusses this problem: "Even when
sexual harassment does not succeed in driving women out of
training and jobs, it inevitably damages their career potential,
undermines their self-esteem, siphons energy away from job performance, and creates serious, extended obstacles to motivation
and ambition."[3]

Whereas it may not be the norm, there are also many tragic
examples of how sexual harassment problems have actually ruined a woman's career. Consider the story of what happened to
Carmita Wood, an administrative assistant in one of Cornell University's major laboratories. "Less than one year after assuming
her new duties, Wood was driven out by a pattern of sexual harassment from an extremely well-placed Cornell official. The New
York State Unemployment Board denied her unemployment
compensation and circumstances militated against an EEOC lawsuit. . . . She went on to expose the abuse by talking about her
own case and making herself an example . . . but the controversy
created as a result of this stand cost her dearly. Job possibilities
dwindled to zero. . . . Although her family has lived in Ithaca for
generations, Carmita Wood eventually had to leave. . . . Unable
finally to find an acceptable job, she applied for unemployment
insurance. She was denied insurance benefits because her rea-

sons for leaving her job were termed merely 'personal' and 'non-compelling.' "[4]

Well, enough of sad tales of woe. Let's figure out how not to let ourselves become casualties of sexual harassment. To help with that very thing, here are some specific situations that professional women are most likely to encounter and some ways you might possibly handle them.

Those Little Love Pats That You Hate

Some people spend thousands of dollars attending encounter groups in which they learn how to touch one another. To get first-hand experience in this sensitive area, all one really has to do is visit a typical business office. Men have been perfecting this touching art for years. Needless to say, it rubs many women the wrong way.

The pervasiveness of sexual harassment has its basis in the way men regard touching and pinching. For many of them, it falls into the category of Boys Will Be Boys—an expected perk of being an executive. Men generally think that a simple pinch or come-on is appropriate behavior; to them it's all in the nature of fun. Most can't comprehend that a woman would really be so offended that she would file a lawsuit in federal court.

So how should a woman best deal with this pressing problem? Here are a few handy suggestions:

1. The straightforward approach. Sharon Steinberg, a highly respected research biologist, found that every time the director of her lab approached her, he put his arm around her or touched her on the hands. She was never certain if he was just a very friendly, tactile sort, but this laying on of hands made her very uncomfortable. Finally, in her scientific, no-nonsense fashion, she told him that although she was certain that he was just being friendly, she didn't feel comfortable in a professional relationship with so much familiarity. Her approach, tactful and firm, worked beautifully with him.

2. Apply a liberal interpretation of the Golden Rule: do unto them as they have done unto you. Lynne Andersen, associate publisher of *The New Mexico Business Journal,* has found the following to be a very effective way to stop office molesters. "When I responded to being patted on the fanny by patting their fanny, the men saw the humor in the situation and immediately left me alone."

3. *The one-liner approach.* After being squeezed just once too often by one office pest, I suggested that if he got his kicks by squeezing things, he should audition for an ad for Charmin toilet tissue and be the Mr. Whipple of his block. He seemed so surprised by my irreverent approach that he left me alone from then on.

The above are relatively successful and seemingly simple solutions. Let's look at some that are a little more complicated.

4. *Start your own "hands-off" policy.* Some men think that it is expected behavior to touch every female within a fifty-mile radius. It is your responsibility to remove their hands.

If you are dealing with a man who may not realize how offensive this touching is to you, simply explain it to him. Gently tell him that his constant touching feels like a power symbol to you and makes you feel like a subordinate. Very politely let him know that you are certain that this was not his intention and that you just wanted to let him know how you felt.

If he truly does understand your discomfort, he will leave you alone in the future and may even thank you for explaining it to him. If he really is an ogler, then you will have to take more drastic measures.

5. *Stop it before it goes any further.* Sometimes women just put up with touching, thinking it relatively harmless. That's what Arlene Czerwinski, a software expert in a New York–based computer firm, did. Unhappily, she discovered that touching was her boss's way of testing how receptive she was for bigger and better things. He interpreted her ignoring the situation as interest, and her ignorance turned out to be anything but blissful. He began coming on stronger and stronger until he finally confronted her with the ultimatum: "Sleep with me or I'll make sure you don't get another job in the computer industry." She refused and was fired by this influential man on the basis of alleged incompetence. Disaster probably could have been averted had she seen the handwriting on the wall and acted early.

6. *Band together—there's safety in numbers.* This technique is particularly useful for lower-level jobs, but believe me, I have seen it work for high-powered executives as well. In a newspaper office where I once worked, the managing editor had an initiation

rite he used on every new female reporter. As she was working at breakneck speed to finish a deadline, he would sneak up behind and put his hands on her breasts and coyly ask, "Guess who?" Frequently he would call a woman reporter into his office and, as he was giving her an assignment, give himself a cheap thrill by pressing against her in a very unpleasant way. He didn't discriminate in this second charming little game: he pressed into service the most senior female reporters as well as the new one. The women reporters decided to take group action. First of all we went to see the editor-in-chief, who was relatively sympathetic; then, to make certain we got results, we went to see the publisher. It worked, I am happy to report. We figured they would have had a tough time firing all of us. If they had, it was clear that we had grounds for taking legal action.

Don't Let Them Call You Sweetheart

Being called pet names is one of my pet peeves. Words like "honey" and "sweetie" are not signs of endearment. I am never sweet to someone who has called me "sweetie." It's demeaning, humiliating, and certainly unprofessional.

HOW TO HANDLE THIS NAME-CALLING

Sticks and stones may break my bones, but if you call me a name, I'll call you one right back. What's in a name, you ask? The answer is, "Plenty!" If you get called "sweetie," feel free to respond in kind. Eileen Shanahan, former undersecretary of the Department of Health, Education and Welfare, retaliates against the name-calling putdown by "coming back with some really outrageous term of endearment. Like, 'OK, lamb chop.' " She reports that this is a successful technique. "It can work. It can make them think about something they haven't thought about."[5]

Use the direct approach and explain why the practice upsets you. Sometimes people use certain words by force of habit. It could be that the men in your office who call you "honey" and other offensive names aren't even conscious that what they are saying is demeaning. Betty Lehan Harragan therefore suggests that you "take the offender aside and explain that such words have bad associations for you, that you think of overeager clerks in a cheap store, and of course you wouldn't want to identify him with such unsophisticated people."

Answer "girl talk" with "boy talk."   As long as men are men and girls are girls, equality in the office will be impossible to obtain. Again, many men just don't think, and may call you a girl because they have often thought of all women as "girls." Here's the way Stephanie Wance, a lawyer, handled this situation:

When a male co-worker stepped into a meeting of women lawyers who were working on a very important case, he remarked, "You girls certainly are doing a good job."

Stephanie looked him right in the eyes (in her best prosecuting attorney fashion) and answered, "Well, we try to keep up with you boys." He got the point!

Sweating Out Locker Room Conversation

Men have been in the corporate ballgame alone for so long that they are terrified that women may cramp their style. Many times a woman is denied a job in an "old boys" department because she might interfere with the all-important male rituals of swearing, telling dirty jokes, and other boyish fun.

What's the best way to handle this problem? Consider some of the following solutions that many of the professional women I interviewed swear by:

1. Humor them.   If humor comes easily to you, it is often the best response. Many of the men that I interviewed reported that they thought too few businesswomen had any sense of humor. Here is your way of proving them wrong.

Dr. Estelle Ramey has an irreverent sense of humor, and she explains how she used it to her best advantage when she was appointed to a scientific study committee.

"When I arrived, everyone was so overly polite—you know, the type of good manners that people show to inferiors. You could tell they were uneasy because they were concerned that they wouldn't be able to tell the same type of jokes. It was a type of psychological discrimination. They knew my scientific credentials. If I had been a man, there would have been none of this stuff. They were not seeing me as a scientist but as a woman scientist, and therefore as someone who was going to be a pain in the ass. You could sense them thinking, 'The next thing you know, they are going to send in a black or a hermaphrodite.' "

Ramey handled this situation with her characteristic humor by suggesting that the men "relax, because I wasn't going to do anything peculiar that they hadn't seen in their bedrooms." This remark seemed to break the ice and helped her win acceptance into this skeptical group.

2. *Tell them an off-color joke right back, but be careful the joke's not on you.* Lynne Andersen and many other women I interviewed felt the best approach in this situation is to simply tell a sexual joke of your own. As she puts it, "I know enough jokes that put men down that I can come right back with a joke that they are the butt of." Andersen and others report that men often see the humor in this and instead of being offended accept it in stride.

However, this approach can have some unpleasant consequences when the double standard rears its ugly head. Men who have offended you with the most disgusting jokes may suddenly become very moralistic and declare that you aren't ladylike if you respond with their type of raunchy humor. Consider this example about a female lawyer's experience:

"When I first went to work there, the office lunch ritual was unbelievable. The men would do nothing except gross out women. The language was not to be believed. I expressed my displeasure and explained how destructive it was. . . . Then about one month later two more women were hired. They got the lunch treatment and one day when a man walked by in real tight pants, one of these women exclaimed, 'Wow, look at that basket!' She was just retaliating and trying to show them, but the men went crazy. They couldn't see it at all and came down on her real hard for being unladylike. She left after a year and I'm sure one of the reasons was this sex thing."[6]

3. *Use the direct approach.* If directness is your style, you might heed the advice in *The Ambitious Woman's Guide to a Successful Career* and react in the following ways when you encounter a remark that you consider sexist:

"Don't be quick to charge discrimination. That usually will put a man on the defensive. . . . Request that the person who made the remark explain what he meant. . . . If you can keep him fishing for words and reasons long enough, you may not have to charge him with bias; it may dawn on him without your active help.

"You can be direct without necessarily sounding bitter or hostile. For example: 'Why do I have the feeling you said that because I am a woman?' "[7]

Of course, this entire approach assumes that you are dealing with an unconscious sexist who would really like to be enlightened.

4. When stronger measures are called for.   There are some men who, unfortunately, don't want to be instructed on how a female co-worker would like to be treated. This type thinks nothing of uttering senseless sexist remarks. Indeed, thinking doesn't seem to be much of a burden at all.

To cite an example, take the experience of Helen Birch, who has a Ph.D. in marine biology and studies the behavior of bottle-nosed dolphins. Her male colleagues like nothing better than to bait her, call her a woman's libber, or tell dirty jokes in her presence. If she protests (which she does daily), they coolly inform her that their little "fun and games" is just part of the male culture. To add a little injury to their insult, they tell her that it is *her* hang-up if she gets upset by it. The following remarks are typical of the abuse she puts up with daily. See if the scenario sounds familiar.

Your male co-workers' conversation is peppered with comments such as "You sure have a cute ass," or "Boy, she certainly has a terrific pair of jugs."

You are continually being subjected to replays of your boss's last evening's sexual scorings. You could not possibly care less.

You have just heard a speech by a brilliant female speaker. Your co-worker sneers and says, "Who cares if she can talk! All I care about is 'Is she good in bed?' "

You are constantly being bombarded with dirty jokes that are degrading to women. Besides being insulting, most of them aren't even funny.

These remarks, which Helen found difficult to deal with, might have been handled in any one of the following ways:

Don't stand for it (or sit for it, for that matter).   Don't be a willing audience. When someone begins to tell off-color jokes or says something derogatory about a female co-worker, simply walk away. It's hard to have a show without the audience.

Get the last laugh by not laughing at all.   Don't encourage the office Don Rickles by laughing at his jokes. Chuckling at stories that are demeaning to women isn't funny.

Embarrass them. Emphasize how childish you think these jokes are by remarking, "My eight-year-old son told me that joke."

Casting Aspersions on the Casting Couch—If Someone Wants to Sleep With You and You Aren't Interested

Casting couches are not just the creation of old B movies. Modern-day Casanovas, in their three-piece suits, still make demands of their women associates; their methods may be more sophisticated and their approach couched in subtler terms, but their wants are the same. You needn't, however, cast your lot with them. Sleeping with someone is never part of your job unless your job is that of a call girl.

As Peggy Kohl, former vice-president of consumer affairs for General Foods Corporation, explains: "You never have to do anything in business (sexually) that you wouldn't do as a private individual."

No, Thanks, I Never Give at the Office—How to Fend Off Unwelcome Advances

Sooner or later a man you work with may proposition you. How are you going to handle him? It pays to be prepared. Let's examine a few situations and the best ways to deal with them.

THE CASUAL PROPOSITION

A male on the prowl is often trite in his approach. The following lines are so frequent that they suffer from indecent overexposure.

◇ "As long as we have such a close working relationship, why don't we extend it to after-hours?"

◇ "What harm could it possibly cause for us to have a casual affair? Nobody else will ever have to know."

◇ "You know, you are so easy to talk to. My wife doesn't understand anything about the business world, and frankly, lately doesn't understand me too well."

Although these lines are all somewhat different, they have one thing in common: The men aren't coming on too strong and are just casually suggesting a sexual fling. Here are some ways you might turn them down without permanently turning them off:

1. The good humor lady—one-liners that will put them back in line. If humor is your style, sometimes the best approach is to leave 'em laughing. If a man starts coming on to you, start coming on like Dorothy Parker.

For example, when a male colleague suggests we head for his apartment or the Shady Lane Motel, I act horrified and reply, "Well, I have certain minimal standards for my affairs. If we can't go to the Plaza Hotel in New York, then we won't go anywhere." This method is particularly effective if you live in California.

Lynne Andersen notes an added benefit of treating a proposal with humor. "Humor gives the man a way out. It's not like he's been rejected. It makes it seem like he was joking, too. This way everybody's dignity is saved."

2. The honest-but-flip approach. At a meeting of statisticians, Brenda Foster was approached by a man who asked if she were interested in coming to his room. Foster, a calculating statistician, dealt with the situation in this manner: "I am not particularly interested in sleeping with you." Whipping out her calculator and doing some quick figuring, she continued, "However, if my statistical sampling is correct, I have estimated that there are probably eighty female statisticians here; approximately fifteen of them are probably very horny. The chances are 19 percent that you could get one of them to sleep with you."

3. The direct-and-open way. Merily Keller, a public relations consultant in Austin, is the honest type of woman who is not comfortable using humor to bail her out of situations. Whenever she is approached by a man who wants to extend his public relations into the private domain, she is direct, calm, and honest. "It's not always necessary or appropriate to be funny. I am a very open person and say what I think. Therefore I explain to a man, 'I'm interested in being a friend and talking to you, but I'm not into that other scene.'"

4. Tact is back—be so charming they'll never realize you are saying no. Marlene Sanders uses the following smooth tactic that leaves the fragile male ego intact. When someone propositions her at work, she replies diplomatically: "Look, I haven't got any moral objections, but I think it's a bad practice to get involved with anybody in the office. I think you are a charming guy, and if you only worked somewhere else, maybe I could be enticed, but it's just my policy."

5. My heart belongs to another. Jo Foxworth thinks that the only answer that a man can accept without embarrassment is 'There's somebody else!' The pressure usually stops cold when you explain that your husband or lover is wildly jealous and would murder any man who so much as looked at you."[8]

6. *Explain it would ruin your working relationship.*   Susan, an actuary in a major insurance company, confided the following story to me after I assured her "my policy" would be not to mention her name. When her boss announced that he wanted their relationship to extend to after-hours, she calmly answered that she couldn't. To this "high-risk" offer, she explained, "I feel that having an affair with you might jeopardize the fine business relationship we have. Since I take my work so seriously and I know you do too, I don't think either of us wants to risk any involvement."

7. *Ignorance can be bliss—pretend you don't understand what's going on.*   Margaret Henning and Anne Jardim suggest the clever ploy of pretending you don't understand what games are being played. "The first and best strategy is not to engage the issue at all. You don't see it, hear it, understand it. You are so preoccupied with the job to be done that you tend to respond to a come-on with 'How much is your area going to be overbudget this month?' Think through ahead of time a series of task-related responses you can make in these situations."[9]

8. *Don't always consider it an insult.*   Keep in mind that many men feel obligated to proposition you. According to Michael Korda, this tendency is just part of the macho male conditioning. "At the back of their minds is the fear that a woman may think less of a man if he doesn't at least put up a formalized show of public interest, a kind of gesture to the gallery. Most men do not expect response."[10]

Serious Forms of Sexual Harassment—"Put Out or Get Out"

Casual propositions are one thing, but what do you do about the serious types of harassment that can cost you your job? These incidents are becoming so common that they have drifted down into soap operas. Erica, the beautiful and ambitious heroine of "All My Children," was given the following choice: a producer informed her that if she didn't sleep with him her plans for a TV and movie career were finished.

Upon occasion, life imitates soap operas. If you are presented with an ultimatum that you either sleep with the man or you will be fired or ruined in your industry, it is no time for soft-soaping the issue. There is something that you can do about this problem other than to feel humiliated. Sexual harassment should never be tolerated; you have the right to complain and to take action. Here are some possible options on how to handle this odious problem:

Quitting. If you can easily get another job in a comparable or more prestigious company, by all means do so. This is certainly the easiest and perhaps least emotionally draining of the choices. However, as you know, until you have a new job, it's not a smart idea to quit your original one. Unless you are an heiress or have a limitless savings account, ask yourself if you can actually afford to quit your present position.

Confrontation. Muffet Foy Cuddy suggests that you inform the harasser in clear, simple statements that his/her attentions are not wanted. If possible, do this in front of witnesses. Deal with the harassment as directly and firmly as you possibly can.

Complaining. "If he/she persists after receiving your state-ment," Mrs. Cuddy says, "report the problem to your supervi-sor. If the harasser is your supervisor, someone authorized to take personnel actions affecting you or someone who can influ-ence personnel actions, a more serious threat is presented to your job.

"You need to take specific steps to protect yourself. Document the incident or incidents. Collect copies of progress reports, per-sonnel files and anything that shows your good work record. Do this before you complain. In retaliation, your boss may remove any favorable reports from your files and give poor performance reports.

"It is extremely important to take accurate notes of what is said or done. Record the date, the time, the place, and the names of witnesses if there are any. Do not go into an office or any other place for a one-on-one discussion. Bring a witness or a tape re-corder to any meeting. Tape recorders are admissable evidence at the administrative level of review, though not in court. Talk to your co-workers about the incident. Find out whether other women have had similar experiences with the same man or others in the company. If you feel that reporting to your supervisor will do you harm, report directly to your company CEO.

"If you are not satisfied with the resolution of your complaint within the department or you have been fired for refusing sexual advances, contact your state Civil Rights or Human Rights Office or, the Equal Employment Opportunity Commission (within 180 days of the incident) about filing a charge of sex discrimination.

"Bring your notes and any documentation with you. You will need the support of witnesses willing to testify or other women who have been similarly treated. Keep notes of all events relating to the reported incident and to any others which may occur in retaliation for having made a charge. If you are suddenly transferred to a lower-paying job or passed over for promotion, report this to management. If you have already filed a charge with the State Civil Rights or Human Rights Office or with the Federal EEOC, contact them about filing a retaliation charge.

"If you have been physically harassed or threatened while on the job, you may also have grounds for criminal charges of assault and battery. Contact an attorney or the police."

Advice on which course of action to take.   Since the course of action you choose in a sexual harassment case could affect the rest of your life, be certain you know exactly what you are doing. This is serious business. I suggest you seek advice from people well versed in this area, who can counsel you on the best route to take:

a. Your own private attorney.
b. A local women's center.
c. The American Civil Liberties Union. This group can provide attorneys or refer you to attorneys who handle Title VII cases.
d. Groups to write, call, or go see for support:

   1. The Working Women Institute (against Sexual Harassment)
   593 Park Avenue
   New York, NY 10021
   (212) 638–3143
   This is a clearinghouse on the issue of sexual harassment. They maintain a library of legal briefs on the subject and refer callers to lawyers and discussion groups in their own area.
   2. Alliance Against Sexual Coercion
   P.O. Box 1
   Cambridge, MA 02139
   (617) 547–1176

3. Nine to Five Office Workers
140 Clarendon Street
Boston, MA 02116
(617) 536–6003

4. Center for Women Policy Studies
Suite 508
2000 P Street NW
Washington, DC 20036
(202) 872–1770

5. Action Against Sexual Harassment in Education and Employment
P.O. Box 1491
Madison, WI 53701

6. ACLU Women's Rights Project
132 West Forty-third Street
New York, NY 10036
(212) 944–9800

7. YWCA U.S.A.
600 Lexington Avenue
New York, NY 10022
(212) 753–4700

8. Women Organized Against Sexual Harassment
300 Eshelman Hall
University of California
Berkeley, CA 94702
(415) 642–7310

9. Women Office Workers
680 Lexington Avenue
New York, NY 10022
(212) 688–4160

10. Wider Opportunities for Women
1325 G Street NW
Washington, DC 20005
(202) 638–3143

In addition to the above, an excellent source of detailed information on the topic is the book *Sexual Shakedown* by Lin Farley.

Role Reversal—Sexual Harassment of Men by Women

Before we leave this subject behind us, I must at least mention that sexual harassment isn't always restricted to men trying to manipulate women into having affairs with them. One way women are gaining equality, it seems, is in the touchy area of sexual harassment. Harassment by females certainly is not the norm, and women are not threatening their male subordinates in record-breaking numbers, but it is happening.

For example, a reliable source in Washington, DC, recounts the following experience. A man, an attractive, sexy Washington economist, was trying to get money together to start a new consulting firm. In the course of this endeavor, he went to a well-known philanthropist who agreed to lend him the money. His liaison was a female lawyer who was supposed to take care of all the details. One of these details she assumed was a pleasant affair with this charming economist. But, while he was certainly no Joseph Andrews, he wasn't really interested in sleeping with her, either.

She was furious and got her sweet revenge by seeing to it that he didn't get the needed money for his project. Furthermore she cut him dead socially, and he stopped receiving invitations to parties where he could have met the necessary contacts for his new enterprise.

It goes without saying that this type of manipulation is every bit as bad as what men have been doing to women for years.

On the Other Hand, What If You Want to Say Yes?

It may seem as if I am going from the sublime to the ridiculous in turning from serious sexual harassment to situations where you might want to become involved with someone in your office. However, although the situations might appear as diametrically opposed as the philosophies of Norman Mailer and Gloria Steinem, they are in fact both very real problems that professional women are faced with in today's complicated working world. Let's examine some of these problems and discuss the pros and cons and some possible consequences of each.

Tackling the most difficult and controversial situation first, what *about* the office affair? Should you or shouldn't you? To help you with this decision, consider first the following advantages reported to me by professional women in the know.

ADVANTAGES OF THE OFFICE AFFAIR

The office is the best place to meet men.   As Lynne Andersen explained to me, "Where else are you going to meet men who are your equals? Nice loving relationships are hard to find these days. It would be absurd to exclude all the men at work!"

Familiarity breeds companionship.   Many women pointed out that they enjoy being involved with men at work because they "have so much in common." As one executive put it, "If the chemistry is there and you also have the bond of work, it can enrich the relationship that much more."

An office affair can enhance working relationships.   In the book *Getting Yours*, a woman lawyer discusses her office affairs: "Neither of us were playing status games and the sexual intimacy enhanced our working relationship in the law firm. We paid closer attention to one another's sensitive spots as well as to our ideas."[11]

You might even meet your prince at work—now wouldn't that be charming?   Sometimes life imitates fairy tales and it seems at many offices love is a perk of a high-powered position. In an article entitled "In Defense of The Office Romance" (*Savvy*, May 1982), it is reported that "Cupid is working on company time. Love is blooming in the hothouse corporate climate of the Eighties, where ambitious, intelligent, and attractive men and women pursue common goals, share mutual interests, and spend most of their waking hours getting to know one another. . . . The thrill of achievement, the heady high of common goals make the office the natural scene of love in the Eighties."

So perhaps you can meet in the boardroom, fall in love on the corporate jet, and ride into the sunset on two expense accounts.

DISADVANTAGES OF THE OFFICE AFFAIR

"It's very difficult to run an army if the general is in love with the sergeant."
                                                                    Margaret Mead

On the negative side of the ledger there are, needless to say, some disadvantages you should consider.

You may lose more than your reputation—you may lose your job. Nowhere is the double standard in the business world more pervasive than in the sexual arena. A man will put a few more notches in his executive scoring belt while you'll, no doubt, get fired.

It is arduous to maintain a businesslike relationship with your boss, co-worker, or male secretary when you are having an affair with him. It's even worse after you break up. Imagine trying to negotiate a raise with or give orders to a man with whom you have stopped sleeping. Never will you feel more like an underling!

LOVE MAY MAKE THE WORLD GO 'ROUND, BUT IT MAKES THE OFFICE GO TO HELL—THE EFFECT OF YOUR AFFAIR ON THE OFFICE

You may want people talking about you, but you don't want them gossiping. It's almost impossible to keep an office affair clandestine. People sometimes talk about you even when you are perfectly innocent. You may, for example, have seen the episode of "The Mary Tyler Moore Show" when Ted Baxter, the bumbling anchorman, was trying to impress his colleagues with his imaginary affair with Mary. Mary, who was furious and embarrassed, protested, "Now everyone in this building thinks I am easy pickings. The man at the newsstand called me 'Hi Cookie,' and the elevator man stopped between floors and announced, 'We are out of gas, Toots.' "

To paraphrase Mary's predicament, it is almost impossible to keep on a professional footing with other workers when you have become their favorite topic of conversation during coffee breaks. You may find that instead of being treated like a well-respected executive, you are scorned like Hester Prynne.

Betty Lehan Harragan notes that "Male subordinates who are equal colleagues of the offending woman will hate her for taking 'unfair advantage' of her sexual attraction. Other women will also hate her for much the same reasons. Her boss's superiors will automatically classify her as a sex-servicing instrument, not a candidate for recognition on her own merits." [12]

Being in an office where two co-workers are in love is anything but lovely. When I worked as a copywriter in Atlanta, I was on a big account with an art director and a creative supervisor who were having an affair. Since they were mercurial lovers, their colleagues, in self-defense, were always having to gauge their emotional temperatures. Half the time, being around these two was akin to having front row seats at the title fight of the battle between the sexes. The rest of the time, when they weren't actively involved in battle, they were equally impossible. They totally forgot where they were and acted like two love-starved kids in an early Sandra Dee movie. It was embarrassing, unprofessional, and decidedly inefficient. It took the three of us a month to finish a project that should have taken a week.

I've got a secret.   The leaks in Watergate are dribbles in comparison to the ones that show up in office romances. Therefore, if you do have an office secret (including confidential company information), don't tell it to someone who you know is involved in an affair unless you want his or her lover to know also. As Merily Keller warned, "People who are lovers tend to tell each other everything. If you told X, his lover would also find out."

IF YOU ARE DETERMINED TO CARRY ON AN AFFAIR, DO IT
DISCREETLY

If, in spite of the possible consequences, you are madly in love and are having an affair with a man in your office, don't broadcast it to the world. Be discreet and remember to keep your love life and your work life separate. Be mature and professional.

A Summary—Travel at Your Own Risk—Don't Be a Casualty of the Transition Period

It's the best of times. It's the worst of times. It's the most confusing of times.   Although these may be the best times in history to be a working woman, they may also be the most confusing. For instance, on the subject of office affairs, women are getting mixed signals. Most of us were raised to believe it was never a good idea to get involved with a man you worked with. Upbringing dies hard. Therefore, when fashionable magazines issue such statements as, "the rule used to be 'Don't play around in the Corporation.' But there is no code anymore," we are bound to feel some conflict.

We are living in a transition period where we constantly receive conflicting signals and advice. The problem in general reminds me of the lines from *The Sun Also Rises* in which Jake, the
Hemingway hero, is trying to figure out the values of his changing society. He muses to himself: "That was morality; things that
made you disgusted afterward. No, that must be immorality."

Perhaps our conflict isn't quite so dramatic, but how do we
decide our right conduct in a world where the rules are changing
as quickly as the headlines? On this subject my advice is to use
your own discernment and good sense. How you act may depend
upon the type of office you work in. The rules of conduct in a
creative advertising agency are different from those in a staid
banking firm. Consider next your personal moral code. Finally,
what have been the rewards and problems for others in your
company who have had office affairs? How will the way you conduct yourself affect your career?

Err on the side of caution. I feel that the business world is
still basically conservative and most of the men controlling the
business community tend to be somewhat old-fashioned in their
moral judgments. This is not to say that they haven't been having
affairs with their secretaries for years, but many still cling to the
double-standard mode of behavior when it comes to their female
co-workers. So travel at your own risk!

CASUAL AND INNOCENT BUSINESS OUTINGS

Every business woman must learn how to keep her professional footing at a harmless lunch or a pleasant evening out with
her boss, co-worker, or client. Here's some specific advice on
this sometimes tricky business:

*Help! How to handle sticky situations without getting
stuck.* Your boss asks you for drinks and dinner. Up till now,
your relationship has been strictly businesslike. Should you go?
If you have no reason to believe that your boss is a philanderer
and you would enjoy a harmless evening out with him, then by
all means say yes.

If, on the other hand, you feel that your boss plans a brief affair
instead of going over some briefs, then you need to be on your
guard. You could merely state quite casually that you are busy.
This technique will obviously become a little suspect after ten

times, but it's good for a few invitations. Or, if you and your boss have a good rapport, why not level with him? Be your most diplomatic self and explain how you enjoy working with him and value your working relationship. Continue by saying you just wouldn't feel quite right about seeing him after hours and that your job is so important to you, you wouldn't do anything to jeopardize it.

How to say yes to dinner without ending up as the dessert. If you aren't certain how innocent the business dinner is really going to be, here are some safeguards to make certain the mood doesn't become amorous.

Pick the place. Obviously you don't want to rendezvous at Hernando's Hideaway or some intimate little bistro designed for cozy tête-à-têtes. Likewise, don't go to any restaurant that has a motel attached. Hotels are generally safer, but if you are really feeling cautious, you might stay away from any "inn" place. Finally, don't go to the spot (if there is one) where all the company lovers hang out; that's like sending out an invitation to an affair.

Regulate the conversation. By this, I don't mean you have to act as formally as if you were attending a formal business meeting. Instead, keep it light. This might actually be a good time to get to know your boss better. It's certainly permissible to chat about a few things that are not strictly shop talk. It could be that you both share a love of the theatre, art museums, and boa constrictors. It's fine to be friendly, but don't encourage intimate conversation. If you see it heading that way, quickly bring up a business matter.

Dress in an attractive but businesslike outfit. Save your sexy clothes for someone you want to seduce.

Don't drink too much. You need to keep a clear head if you want to maintain your professional image.

Set a time limit and stick to it. Before the evening begins, explain that you have to be home by a given time. No excuse is really necessary, but saying "I have some work to catch up on" has a nice touch.

Put yourself in the driver's seat—take your own car. A dangerous route to follow is to allow your male colleague to drive you home in his car or to accompany you in a taxi. This could be your road to ruin since it is a small step between the car and the door to your bedroom.

We must have lunch sometime! Counter his dinner invitation with lunch. If a man suggests going out for dinner, tell him you would prefer lunch; this hour is always safer. As Beverly Lann-quist explains, "If I thought someone was asking me to dinner because that was the first step leading to an affair, then I wouldn't go. I would say, 'Gee, what about lunch?' You can't get into as much trouble over lunch."

Eileen Shanahan has some appetizing ideas on how to keep your business lunch "strictly business." When you are asked to lunch, Shanahan suggests answering with, " 'Oh, and why don't we invite Phil Jones because you know he is involved in that problem, too.' He can't really say no, since he's pretending that this is all about business. If you really think you should go, and you can't get out of it, the very fact that you have suggested that somebody else come with you implants in his mind the idea that you're not on the prowl for an affair."[13]

HOW TO REMAIN FRIENDS WITH THE MEN YOU WORK WITH WITHOUT IT GETTING TOO FRIENDLY

There is, happily, something between the office affair and an impersonal business relationship: it's called friendship. A superb role model for "being just friends" with men at work was de-picted in the old "Mary Tyler Moore Show." Mary, Lou, and Murray were like a close-knit family. They loved and respected each other, but there were never any sexual implications about their relationship. They hugged and were warm with each other in a healthy, positive way. But that's as far as it ever went.

I, too, was a very good friend of Carlos and Charles, my part-ners in our advertising agency, and with David, my associate co-pywriter. Besides working under close and pressurized condi-tions, we had lunch, drinks, and often dinner together. We traveled together and sometimes worked side by side till 3 A.M. Many times I saw more of them on a given day than I did of my hus-band. However, there was never a thought of a sexual innuendo between any of us. We were basically professional co-workers and very dear friends.

Obviously attaining this type of friendship depends upon your presenting yourself in a certain manner: warm and friendly but never seductive. When you start sending out sexual signals, it's hard to remain pals. In this context, of course, I am talking about sensitive men who value platonic female companionship. This type of relationship requires that you choose your office friendships carefully.

SOME SWIFT TIPS SO YOU DON'T FEEL LIKE THE STAR OF "GULLIBLE'S TRAVELS"

It would be guileful of us to think that sex will play no part in our business traveling. First and foremost, when most of us travel, we become different people. We are no longer living in a nine-to-five world, our families are a long way away, and we are headed for a possible adventure. Carolyn Meyer, a writer who travels throughout the country for research and promotional purposes, describes her transformation when she is on the road. "I find personally that my life changes totally when I travel. My reflexes change, my adrenalin is up. I actually am not the same person. It seems as if all my connections to my home and family are broken."

Dr. Jet Set and Mr(s). Hyde—the metamorphosis of both the male and female business traveler.   On one of my frequent trips to New Orleans while working for American International Pictures, I was accompanied by a male co-worker. This man had been a paragon of virtue in the office, but began to transform as we boarded the plane. His inhibitions seemed to shed with every mile that we soared. He revealed his secret lust for me, kept placing his hand on my leg, and, in general, turned into a veritable lech before my eyes. I spent the rest of the trip hiding from this jet-set Mr. Hyde.

Although I have no statistics to prove me right, I suspect this metamorphosis is a predominately male phenomenon. However, women also change their personalities on trips, and while they might not consider having a liaison with someone in their home office, they might think about playing around a little on a trip. Recently a man and a woman told me travel stories about the opposite sex that sounded so similar that, for our purposes, I have condensed them here into one quote: "Men (women) who are normally considered very family-oriented, true-blue individuals would go on trips with me, and suddenly they were all on the make. They had a completely different set of rules that they used when they traveled."

We have to start meeting like this.   In a positive context, trips can be marvelous opportunities to meet interesting people. So if you are gregarious but discreet, don't always pass up the chance to say hello to the person next to you on the plane, or smile at a man at the next table at a restaurant. You never know what you might be missing.

For example, on a recent trip to Montreal I happened to sit next to a man who turned out to be an important editor. Partly because of this accidental meeting, I was given one of the best free-lance writing assignments I have ever had.

However, my pièce de résistance was on the trip on which I met my husband. I was in Chapel Hill, North Carolina, setting up a movie premiere; he was a professor at Duke. We both were having a drink in the same bar and struck up an innocuous conversation. Just so you know some modern-day stories still end happily, we recently celebrated our fourteenth wedding anniversary.

How to go for a drink or dinner with a man without having to go any further.   Like much of what we have been discussing, the way you present yourself will depend, to a great extent, on how you wish to be treated. For instance, I am generally very friendly but do not send out inappropriate sexual signals. If you are interested in companionship and fun but nothing more, here are some more tips on nonsexual socializing:

Don't send out mixed signals.   Maxene Fabe, an author who travels frequently on business, "finds that if you go out to dinner with someone, that can be fine. Just make it clear that you merely want to be friends. Don't be flirtatious; just say 'good night' at the door. It's when you give mixed messages that you have problems."

Pay your own way.   Letitia Baldrige, the purveyor of propriety, suggests that if a man wants to join you for drinks and you would like him to, "Make it clear that you will put your own drink on your own bill. However, if he insists on paying for that cocktail and you decide to have one more with him, say firmly, but again with a smile, 'I would like another one, but this time both drinks go on my bill.' He will understand you are not letting him pick you up."

Set up a reason why it will have to be an early evening.   Baldrige advises, "If you decide to eat dinner together, once again you can avoid the possibility of complications later in the evening by stating before dinner that you will pay for your own meal, and by insisting that you are tired and have a lot of work to do—hence it will have to be an 'early evening.' "[14]

Some of the techniques (such as regulating the conversation and dressing in a businesslike fashion) discussed earlier in this chapter under "Casual and Innocent Business Outings" also apply here.

MEETING MEN WHILE TRAVELING

This book is not meant as a primer on how to pick up men. If you want to do extensive research on this subject, I suggest you read *How to Make a Man Fall in Love with You* by Tracy Cabot.

Many women and men find traveling is a good opportunity for some "harmless, no-strings-attached" sex. Again, this is, of course, an individual matter. I personally like strings attached to my sex and enjoy a closed marriage. So I am no expert in this subject. I would advise, however, to let your own good judgment and common sense be your guide. Just be smart and discreet and don't end up as a casualty of casual sex.

"I VANT TO BE ALONE"—TIPS ON HOW NOT TO GET PICKED UP

Some people really have no interest in approaching travel as a contact sport. Perhaps they are exhausted—business traveling in fact can be quite fatiguing! Maybe they are involved in a not-so-open marriage or relationship and could not be less interested in a little fling. Or it could be that they are very private types and are not interested in encounters of any kind. For all of you who fall into any of these categories, here are some ways to imitate Greta Garbo if you "vant to be alone."

Look businesslike. If you follow Baldrige's advice, you will minimize your pickup potential. She notes that "If you are 'on the road,' your briefcase can be your security blanket. If you go into the bar of your hotel or motel for a cocktail, or if you go into the restaurant for dinner, take along your briefcase or some file folders as a conspicuous sign of your business profession. Dress in business or travel attire. . . . The people around you will know by the way you are dressed, by what you are carrying, and by your manner that you are obviously passing through town on business."[15]

Be preoccupied. Men are much less likely to pester you if you look very busy. Therefore, look totally absorbed in a book. Sherri Van Saxon, marketing director for the Dallas-based Wyatt Cafeterias, uses this approach on airplanes: "As soon as the plane is airborne, I open my briefcase and get to work. This discourages all the men who feel obligated to make conversation with every woman on the plane. I, for one, do not want to be bothered."

Don't start a conversation. On an airplane or in a café, if you truly do want to be alone, don't make small talk with any of the men around you. They might take it as an overture to bigger and better things. In this case, silence can be golden.

Remember! There's nothing necessarily wrong with being rude—if being alone is what you want. Conditioning may die hard, but forget the genteel training you learned as a little girl. If a man is being obnoxious, tell him to leave you alone. Don't worry about hurting his feelings. You're not running for Miss Congeniality. You have a perfect right to your privacy.

Summary

In short, there are few absolute truths in the area of social conduct. Your main concern, as a businesswoman, is to ensure that you are treated fairly and that you treat others accordingly. With this in mind, if I had to pick one quote as the précis of this chapter, it would be the following one from Beverly Lannquist: "In this area [sexual encounters], like in all other phases of one's business life, it is incumbent upon a woman to act maturely."

6

Time Waits For No Woman

TIMELY TIPS FOR OFFICE AND HOME

"Lost time is never found again." *Benjamin Franklin*

I've been meaning to get around to this chapter for weeks, but I just couldn't seem to find the time. Also, I couldn't quite remember what I had done with all the books telling me how to get organized. I knew they must be somewhere under that mound of papers.

For years I have struggled with finding the perfect solution on how to be brilliantly organized. My favorite fantasy is of being fabulously wealthy, able to hire someone for every chore: a cook, a gardener, a nanny to take care of me, a laundress, a personal hairdresser, an appointment secretary, a downstairs maid, an upstairs maid (which would be the height of luxury in my one-story house), and an all-purpose elf to organize my life. However, unless I am suddenly adopted by a Saudi Arabian oil sheik, I will have to continue with more plebeian ways of dealing with organizational problems.

My younger brother Bob has a rather cavalier method of dealing with the details of his life. He doesn't spend hours plotting out the most efficient way of doing laundry or washing dishes. His solution is simply to transcend all these mundane chores. When he is out of clean underwear, he buys a new month's supply. Rather than figuring out when he will have a moment to take care of those dishes, he tosses out the dirty ones and buys a new set.

For most of us ordinary mortals, however, my brother's method is not entirely practical (except for those who have ready access to an underwear and a dishware factory). For us less frivolous souls there are several more practical things that can be done to make our lives run more smoothly. Let's see how some elementary techniques can be used to make order out of chaos in our everyday lives.

A LITTLE MESS NEVER HURT ANYONE, OR WHY BE ORGANIZED, ANYWAY?

Is there really anything wrong with stumbling through life like a female Oscar Madison? You might be a lot of laughs! But, by the same token, you would probably be laughed out of the executive echelon. Disorganization in the business world is no joking matter and could turn your career into a very brief tragedy. Beverly Lannquist explains: "I don't believe I have ever known anybody who was successful who was not organized."

While it is important for both men and women executives to be organized and able to manage time efficiently, it is particularly crucial for working women. Although most women I know could beat most men hands down in any organizational marathon, women still suffer from being thought of as bubblebrains. Many men still believe that women are chronically late for appointments and that they spend hours fumbling around in messy purses to find an eyebrow pencil—in short, the dizzy dame image. In reality we know that women are paragons of organization and that, as wives and mothers, they've had to learn how to perform organizational juggling acts that could rival anything ever seen on "The Ed Sullivan Show."

As I have reiterated time and again, however, it doesn't matter if this image is true or not so long as it is perceived by others to be true. Dr. Estelle Ramey, in a more eloquent way, observed, "As long as women, as a group, are seen as inadequate compared with men, then every single woman, no matter how successful, is tarred with that brush." With this in mind, let's take a look at how the outside world views you and determine if this image is enhancing or damaging to your executive status.

First of all, is your office neat and organized, so that it reflects well on you? Or does it look about as tidy as Atlanta after Sherman's troops marched through? Do you remember all your busi-

ness appointments and show up promptly? Or is your desk calendar buried under a stack of year-old newspapers? Standing
people up for business dates is a great way to make certain your
career doesn't stand a chance of succeeding!

Are you working longer hours but getting less done? Are you
still working on a report that was due two months ago because
you spend half your days in useless meetings? Is everything you
are doing at work leading toward career advancement or are you
frittering away your time on silly details like whether to buy sil-
ver or gold paper clips?

Are you utilizing your prime time or are you scheduling important appointments at hours when you are totally "out of it"?
Did an important client caustically remark last week that "You
look as if you've gone home for the day"?

Are you assertive enough to say NO to activities that won't
further your career, or are you a hopeless "YES-woman"? Do you
spend hours on a letter to the typewriter repair man, making it
letter-perfect, or do you handle your correspondence quickly and
efficiently? Do you spend half of every day wining and dining
unimportant people at business lunches? These meals may be
going to waist while eating up valuable time!

Are you on time for business appointments? Or do you confirm
that old saw that "women are always late" by arriving breathlessly fifteen minutes after a meeting has started? Some of you
may be putting to good use all the on-the-job training you got in
time management by being wives and mothers. On the other
hand, you may fail to see the correlation between scheduling ballet lessons for Johnny and football practice for Mary with arrang-
ing high-level business meetings. The only difference is that the
office is easier than the home, so the role of an executive should
be duck soup.

Since the way you structure your working day is crucial to your
image as an executive, it's time we helped you become "The Organization Woman."

Office Mess-Takes

Your office says a lot about you. If you can hardly wade through
it because of all the "papers you are going to get to someday," it
doesn't show you are swamped with work; it proves you need to

get organized. Stephanie Winston, in *The Organized Executive,* says that "the key to paper management is *processing:* that is, channeling each piece from your in-box to its appropriate destination. But channel it where? What are your alternatives? . . .

1. *Toss.* 'Man's best friend aside from the dog,' says *Business Week,* 'is the wastebasket.'

2. *Refer.* Delegate paper work when possible to a secretary or staffer, or send it on to a colleague with greater knowledge or expertise in that area. . . .

3. *Act.* Place all papers requiring personal action on your part— dictating a letter, composing a report, analyzing the budget, researching data—into an 'action' box or folder, or on one predesignated spot on your desk. . . .

4. *File.* Set up a box or folder marked 'to file' for your deskside files. . . .

4½. *Read.* Why this 'half' designation for reading, which is, after all, an action? Because any paper that requires more than five to ten minutes of reading time should be handled separately."[1]

Edwin C. Bliss in his valuable book, *Getting Things Done,* feels most people could clear their office in one fell swoop by practicing "Wastebasketry." He advises that you "Be ruthless in channeling paper into the wastebasket instead of into the files."

However, if your wastebasket floweth over, maybe some of the materials that you are depositing there should never have reached your desk in the first place. One of Bliss's suggestions which you should *not* file in your wastebasket, states that "Perhaps your secretary can divert part of the flow directly to the wastebasket, to keep junk mail out of your 'In' box. Ask to have your name removed from mailing lists for little-read periodicals and from the routing list for office correspondence that has no value for you."[2]

I KNOW IT'S IN HERE SOMEWHERE

Filing would seldom appear on anyone's definitive list of life's great pleasures. The only person I ever heard exclaim "Oh frabjous day, it's filing time" is now ensconced in the home for the bemused. Nonetheless, at some point in your office existence you will probably be forced to do some filing. I myself have been waiting for years for a well-organized leprechaun to put every piece of paper I own into its proper place. However, as of now, this leprechaun has been as unreliable as Godot.

You will probably find a similar lack of organizational sprites, so here are some hints to file away in case you have to fend for yourself.

From Edwin Bliss I have learned again that less is more. His motto is, "If in doubt, throw it out." Another of his maxims on this subject is, "A few fat files are better than a lot of thin ones." The rationale here is "the more sub-divisions you have, the more chance there is for misfile . . . it takes a bit longer to go through a fat file to find what you want, but you save more than enough time in filing (and avoidance of errors) to make up for it."[3]

Nothing is more frustrating than trying to remember under what category you filed something. I had a friend who almost lost an analysis account because she couldn't remember where she had placed some vital information. At the zero hour, she finally recalled that she had, but of course, labeled the file "Shirley," because that was the name of the executive secretary of the firm she was dealing with.

Try to find a label that sums up the general concept of the information to be filed—preferably a single word—and mark the folder accordingly.

At least once a week, grit your teeth and file everything in its proper place. If you let it go longer than that, you'll be so intimidated by the size of the stack, you'll never get to it.

KEEP A WELL-ORGANIZED CALENDAR

One of my pet peeves in life is being stood up for a business appointment. It only happens occasionally, however, because it indicates to me that the person in question is either disorganized or very rude. In either case, I won't be bothered a second time. I figure that any person who can't remember to meet me for lunch will probably forget to work on my business projects as well.

To make certain that you are never a no-show, it is imperative that you keep a detailed calendar. As Carol Price, a graphics designer at Los Alamos National Laboratory, explains: "In this job, I have to be extremely organized. Therefore, I keep a good calendar in one central location where I can write down all the important things that I need to do every day."

CLUTTER IS NOT A SIGN OF CREATIVE GENIUS

Whenever you reach the stage where you spend more time looking for papers than working on them, it's time to reorganize your office. The most efficient way of doing this is to place all your papers in a single pile. Quickly go through them (using your wastebasket frequently) and divide them into categories:

1. Top priority
2. Low priority
3. Pending
4. Reading

Put your most pressing item from the first pile in the middle of your desk. Then put everything else away in the appropriate files. You will be tempted to put all your top-priority items on the desk so you can get to them. This is faulty logic, for you can only work on one project at a time.

Speaking of clearing your desk, it's a good idea to clear it or at least generally organize it every night before heading home. I always set out a list of what I want to accomplish the next day so it's the first thing I see when I come to work in the morning.

"Why Don't I Seem to Get Anything Done?"

Sometimes people put in a full day at work and are amazed to discover at the end of it that they have accomplished very little. Efficiency experts estimate that most of us only work three or four productive hours a day. As a result, longer hours are not necessarily better hours. How effectively you work and not how long is what counts. Try some of the following suggestions on how to be more productive:

1. *Good work may be its own reward, but it's more fun to get a present.* You may remember freshman psychology when you studied Skinner boxes and Pavlov's responses. Whether you do or not, you'll be happy to know that some of these techniques can be applied to your own personal rat race. Essentially, the idea is to give yourself a reward after you have done a task. A reward might consist of treating yourself to a nice lunch or even something as trivial as a stick of gum or a piece of candy. Reward yourself for each *small* success, not just for major achievements.

2. *Break, break, break.* You may think you are playing beat the clock by working for long stretches of time without stopping.

But you are only fooling yourself. It is not using time effectively. Your energy level goes down, you begin to get bored, and tension begins to build up. So give yourself a break in one of the following ways:

Stand up and stretch every few hours. Do some relaxation or yoga exercises.

Take a brisk walk around the block or, if that isn't possible, walk around the office.

At breaks, don't think about your work. Bring along something completely diverting to read, such as a mystery, a cookbook, or a travel guide.

Change your routine by standing up for a while.

If you are in a position to do so, hang a "Do Not Disturb" sign on your door and take a quick catnap. If this isn't a possibility, do some deep breathing exercises.

3. *Allow everything to cross your desk only once.*   Take immediate action and you'll be amazed at the time you save.

4. *Delegate authority.*   There is nothing more inefficient than working with someone who wants to be omnipotent. I once worked at a newspaper where the managing editor loved the powerful feeling he got from holding court in his office. Frustrated reporters and advertising managers anxiously lined up, waiting their turn to see the Almighty One. This insecure man felt that no decision, however small, could be made without his input.

People who refuse to delegate authority are not overly conscientious; rather, they are poor managers. Don't try to do everything yourself. It's impossible, inefficient, and a complete waste of your subordinates' time and talents.

5. *Give yourself deadlines.*   Most of us work better under a certain amount of pressure, so that we don't lapse into the Scarlett O'Hara "think-about-it-tomorrow" attitude. Don't succumb to the sin of perfection or you'll spend too much time putting unnecessary finishing touches on work, using the excuse of excellence when actually you are just wheel-spinning. Remember Parkinson's Law: "Work expands to fill the time available for its completion." How to sneak by Parkinson? Give yourself deadlines. Allow only a given amount of time for a task and you will get it done more quickly.

6. *We have to stop meeting like this.*   In an advertising agency where I once served as a copywriter, a weekly ritual was the Monday morning planning meeting. We often spent the first hour

quibbling over who got the last Danish or bagel, and then we launched into our show and tell about our weekend escapades; finally, just before lunchtime we got around to plans for the week. Nothing very worthwhile came out of these meetings because they were time-gobbling events that would have made an efficiency expert shudder.

Anytime you are tempted to call a meeting, ask yourself if it is really necessary. Could you just as well use the telephone and, if you need to, make a conference call? People are much more likely to get off the telephone quickly, whereas they might be inclined to linger around your office. If you discovered that, God forbid, there is no way to avoid having the dreaded meeting, here are some tips on how to make it as painless and as quick as possible:

◇ Start the meeting on time.

◇ Don't bring up irrelevant matters. Stick with the planned agenda.

◇ Try to reach a decision on all items. If that is impossible, always assign responsibility for further action.

◇ Always end your meeting on time.

◇ Sum up at the end of the meeting what was accomplished—what decisions were reached, what assignments were made, when you will meet again. Too many meetings end on a decidedly foggy note, leaving people unclear what took place and who is supposed to do what.

By far the greatest advice I have come across on meetings was given by Robert Townsend. He suggests that to ensure the meeting remains short, have everyone stand up!

7. *Block out your time.*   Aileen Phillips, a consumer affairs specialist, says that her pastime is to head time off at the pass, so it doesn't pass her by. "I've found the following a very good trick which works well for me. If I say from 2:00 to 3:00 I'm going to answer letters, that's the time I allow. I don't run over. And then either I get those things done or I move that slot to the next day. Then, for instance, from 3:00 to 4:00 I go on with my telephone calling or whatever."

This technique also has the added benefit of making you work much faster. In my advertising agency, I wore many hats, so I couldn't afford to dawdle over one project. I would tell myself I had from 9:00 to 10:00 to finish a radio commercial. By the end of the hour, the deed was done.

8. *Concentrate on what you are doing.*   Do one thing at a

time and do it well. If you diffuse your energy by beginning one project, and stopping to work on another, you probably will get nothing done. Give a task your undivided attention before moving on to the next one.

9. *Be decisive.* Robert Townsend feels that common decisions, like when to have the cafeteria open for lunch or what brand of pencil to buy, should be made fast. Otherwise, "the whole organization may be out of business while you oscillate between baby-blue or buffalo-brown coffee cups."

When you are a decision maker, you are bound to make some wrong choices. But so what? Nobody is perfect!

10. *Break difficult tasks into smaller units.* Don't be overwhelmed by the enormity of a huge job. Break it into manageable portions and tackle them one at a time.

11. *Don't get sidetracked—Always keep your objectives in mind.* Townsend has this sage advice on how to train yourself to stay on the right track: "I used to keep a sign opposite my desk where I couldn't miss it if I were on the telephone (about to make an appointment) or in a meeting in my office: 'Is what I'm doing or about to do getting us closer to our objective?' That sign saved me from a lot of useless trips, lunch dates, conferences, junkets, and meetings."[4]

Up-To-The-Minute Advice On How To Save Time

1. *Arrange your business appointments to be in other people's offices, not yours.* It's much easier to get up and leave.

2. *Skip reading the paper at least one morning a week or get up one hour earlier than usual.* Spend the extra time catching up on some work.

3. *If you have the luxury, unplug your phone at work when you don't want to be disturbed.* Ask yourself when was the last time the phone brought you good news.

4. *Don't waste your time and energy on unimportant people and things.*

LISTLESS PEOPLE NEVER GET ANYWHERE

I've never trusted people who don't make lists. I got very nervous recently when a listless person moved into our neighborhood, and I must admit that I live in constant fear that my daughter or son might one day want to marry one. I was certainly relieved, then, to find that most of the women I interviewed shared my great predilection for lists. It restored my faith in humanity.

Laurie Lisle, author of *Portrait of An Artist: The Biography of Georgia O'Keeffe*, listed for me all the different types of lists she keeps: "You basically need to keep a list of what things you have to do within a month, a week, or a year, plus the things you're going to do every day."

Amy Greene, president of Beauty Checkers, confesses to "keeping lists, endless lists, all over the place." She passed on to me the following tip for making being organized more fun. "I keep all my lists in those wonderful little books that are filled with blank pages. I also think it helps you be organized if you always carry a favorite pen."

PRIME TIME

Like Miss Jean Brodie, most us have certain times when we are in our prime. I, for instance, have never had an original thought before 10 A.M. Midnight is when I come alive. Since I was not interested in becoming a lady of the evening or the first female Dracula, I did the next best thing in order to utilize my owlish nature: I became a writer. My husband, on the other hand, is disgustingly cheerful and efficient at 6 A.M.

It's important to identify your prime time and utilize it. You need to do your hardest work at your best time of day. By the same token, schedule your low-priority tasks for your nonprime time.

READING BETWEEN THE LINES

1. Skimming off the top. Even though I hope you don't do it in this book, there really is nothing wrong with not reading every word of certain business materials. Unless you are reading a paper on "Compression Measurement of Neon-Seed Glass Microballoons Irradiated by CO_2 Laser Light," you probably don't need to absorb every word. Skim to get the overall point.

2. Clip an article immediately. Don't waste valuable time trying to remember where you put that pertinent business article you wanted to save. If your magazine collection is as gargantuan as mine, you could save days flipping through every magazine trying to recall which one has the clippable article.

To reduce your confusion, a good tip to put in your clip file is: when first reading a magazine, look at the index page, decide which articles you want to save, and clip them then and there.

3. *Words to read by.* The British critic, F. L. Lucas said, "It is mere common sense never to undertake a piece of work, or read a book, without asking, 'Is it worth the amount of life it will cost?' "

KILLING TIME IS CRIMINAL

Killing time should be a capital offense. So instead of reading a three-year-old copy of *Beauty Shop Digest* in the reception room while waiting for a business appointment, put tidbits of time to good use. Always prepare for the worst and then you won't be frustrated if something goes wrong (as it inevitably will). Always have a book, some work, envelopes to address or birthday cards to send in case your car breaks down or you have to wait for someone. Don't ever be in a position where you have nothing to do but count the increasing lines on your face. You can always make phone calls or even write your weekly "to do" list.

Remember, you are never home free. Bring something you need to do in case your business lunch date is twenty minutes late or you have to wait an inordinately long time at the bank. Always have some work with you—letters to write, a work project to outline, or an upcoming speech to rehearse.

NO, NO, A THOUSAND TIMES NO!

Of all the time-saving techniques ever developed, perhaps the most effective is the frequent use of the word *no*. Some women who were raised to be nonassertive have a great deal of trouble using this word. They are so worried about offending others by not being nice and cooperative that they often spend their lives doing things which are of absolutely no interest to them.

To rid yourself of time-wasting activities, try what Bliss calls "radical surgery." This simply means that you take a hard, cold look at all your activities. Scrutinize your television habits, your telephoning, your social engagements, your reading list, your extracurricular activities, and get rid of everything that doesn't further your career or give you a feeling of accomplishment.

HOW TO DEAL WITH UNWELCOME VISITORS

Every office has a gadfly who flits from office to office making social chit-chat as if he were at a cocktail party. He wants to tell you about his fabulous weekend, his newest technique for stopping smoking (number 555), and the latest antics of his pet skunk. What do you do with this pest, short of muzzling him?

◇ When he walks in, immediately stand up. Don't ask him to sit down.

◇ When he talks to you, answer in bored tones of "uh-huh."

◇ If possible, head him off at the pass. If you see him coming, meet him in the hall. Don't let him in your office. Then you won't have to worry about throwing him out.

◇ Say, "I would certainly like to chat with you, but I have work to do now. Why don't we meet for lunch on _____. Or for a drink. Or during a coffee break." Just make it clear that you do not wish to socialize on office hours.

◇ Suggest that if he has so much leisure time, perhaps he would like to help you tackle some of your work load. Next time he comes in, give him a project or, if that isn't possible, suggest that he help you move the furniture around. That should send him packing.

◇ If you have tried all forms of politeness and his visits have gone on for a long time, then you may have to resort to rudeness. Some people only respond to practically being thrown out of the office.

◇ If nothing else works, go see your supervisor and tell him or her that you aren't getting as much work done as you would like because Mr. Pest keeps bothering you.

If Time Is Money, You Probably Lost a Bundle Today

THE TELEPHONE CONNECTION—A STORY THAT SHOULD HAVE A FAMILIAR RING TO IT

Alexander Graham Bell probably thought that he was bringing an extra measure of sophistication and civilization to the world when he invented the telephone. Boy, did he ever get a wrong number! The telephone may be the salvation of mankind, but it can also be the curse of the working person. To cite a recent example, I rented an office for the exclusive purpose of writing this book, and purposely had no phone installed. While a friend was visiting me a few days ago, I remarked, "Listen to that sound." Somewhat bemused, she replied, "I don't hear anything." To which I replied, "I know. Isn't it wonderful?"

I don't use dial—don't you wish nobody did? Bliss has the following suggestions that have a comforting ring of truth to them:

"*Use a call-back system for phone calls* . . . with calls that don't appear to be emergencies, have your secretary get the name and number so you can call back at your own convenience. . . .

"*By bunching your calls* during a period before lunch or toward the end of the day, when people are less inclined to chat, you can handle calls much more efficiently.

"*Set the tone of the conversation at the beginning.* It's possible to answer the phone in a cordial manner, followed by an inquiry such as 'What can I do for you?' indicating that while you want to be friendly, you also want to be businesslike.

"*Set aside a time for phone calls.* Co-workers understand the need for this kind of arrangement and will not take offense if you explain in advance that you prefer to see people and handle phone calls, for example, before 9:30 and after 11:30, and before 3:00 and after 4:30, thus leaving a substantial block of time in both morning and afternoon to concentrate on major projects."

"*Letters, we get letters, we get tons and tons of letters.*" This title was the theme of the old "Perry Como Show." If you find you're singing the same tune, here are some ways to handle your correspondence that should be followed to the letter.

Bliss's law of correspondence is:

"Handle each letter only once. . . . Do whatever has to be done (checking, forwarding, phoning, replying) immediately, instead of postponing action.

"If a brief reply is possible, write it on the incoming letter or memo, use a photocopy for the file, and return the original to the sender.

"Use form letters and form paragraphs for routine correspondence.

"Don't make frequent revisions. Perfectionism is time-consuming.

"Get to the point.

"For internal correspondence, try 'speedletter' forms with carbons already inserted and with space for a reply.

"Don't write when a phone call will do.

"Use short, terse words. Don't perpetuate polysyllabic obfuscation."

We must have lunch sometime. Business lunches are frequently imperative, but be careful that too many of them aren't eating into your precious time. All too often, business lunches mean that you eat more than you should, drink one too many, and spend a minimum of two hours. By the time you return to your office, you feel weighted down by "lunch lag" and fall into the midafternoon doldrums.

If you are tired of waisting your time, you might substitute a running tab for your lunch bill. Instead of stuffing yourself, trim the fat by playing tennis, going running, or whisking into your neighborhood health spa. You'll feel better, look better, and be a great deal more productive in the afternoon. If you have to talk business during the lunch hour, ask your colleague to go running with you. My husband has been conducting business matters this way for years; he claims that this running start keeps long-winded sales talks to a minimum!

If you need spiritual rather than physical refreshment, take in a museum or a neighborhood art gallery during your lunch hour. If you want to save your after-hours leisure for something considerably more fun than errands, you might want to get those dreary errands polished off during your lunch break.

Time-Honored Tips

"I'M LATE, I'M LATE FOR A VERY IMPORTANT DATE"

Like Alice's White Rabbit, many women still have the unfortunate image of being harebrained and hopelessly late for appointments. If you persist in perpetuating this image, it will be hard for colleagues to take you seriously. People find it anything but cute! So take some timely advice from Jo Foxworth, who says, "Be on time—regardless! As a member of the sex that comedians have cast in a role of eternal tardiness, you can't afford to be late. Ever. As a woman you're expected to be late, but as an executive you're expected to be on time."[5]

Always give yourself ample time to get to an appointment. Allow for the worst—slow traffic, a flat tire, the possibility you won't be able to find a taxi quickly. Nothing makes you feel more frantic than rushing in breathlessly to a business meeting. It certainly doesn't give you the serene image that is likely to make a winning first impression.

If you have trouble with time, buy yourself a timer. Set it to buzz minutes before an important meeting.

DON'T PROMISE MORE THAN YOU CAN DELIVER

Speaking of being on time—and I believe we were—don't put impossible pressures and deadlines on yourself. When my advertising agency was just starting, we were such eager beavers that we would promise completed work in unrealistic time periods. Consequently, we often worked all night to get the work completed. We learned quickly to be more realistic about our deadlines. Nothing turns a client off quicker than a job that isn't done when promised. I am in full agreement with Robert Townsend, who observes, "If asked when you can deliver something, ask for time to think. Build in a margin of safety. Name a date. Then deliver it earlier than you promised.

"The world is divided into two classes of people: the few people who make good on their promises (even if they don't promise as much), and the many who don't. Get in Column A and stay there. You'll be very valuable wherever you are."[6]

I Can't Decide if I Should Make a Decision

One of the greatest time wasters there is, is indecision. If you can't even decide if you should make a decision, you are probably spending far too much time vacillating. Besides wasting time, indecision is an enormous energy drainer. So when you are faced with any decision, big or small, ask yourself, "What's the worst that could happen if I make the wrong decision?"

A bad decision is often better than none. Tell yourself if you never take risks, you will never know the joy of successes. Most decisions aren't made because of fear of mistakes. Procrastination should be viewed as decision by *default*. It's a decision *not to decide*.

DON'T WASTE TIME DOING THINGS YOU DON'T WANT TO DO

I know a woman executive who is a veritable whirling dervish. In her "spare time," she gardens, bakes bread every week, is an accomplished pianist, folk dances, and teaches Sunday school. I once commented that it was nice that she had so many interests that she enjoyed.

She looked at me with amused horror: "Enjoy? I hate doing all those things. What I would really like to do is sit by the fire and read Jane Austen."

"Then why do you do all those activities?"

"Because my husband wants me to bake. My children like the garden. My friends drag me to folk dancing. And the piano and Sunday school are for my mother who's been dead for five years."

The moral of this story is very clear. Live your life for yourself and establish your own priorities. Think of everything you did in the last week. Did you enjoy it? Did it give you a feeling of satisfaction? Did it enrich your life? If it didn't do any of these things, then cut it out. Be ruthless with your time and energy—the present moment will never come again.

Don't waste your time comparing and competing with other people. Figure out the life that is right for you and don't spend precious minutes doing what others expect of you. Evolve your own basic life-style.

Be certain you know your work and personal goals. Otherwise, you will be a pilot with no flight plan and will just keep circling the field instead of feeling well-grounded. Let's take a few minutes to think about goals. Write down your goals for:
◇ The rest of the week
◇ One year
◇ Three years
◇ Five years

Many women aren't conditioned to have long-range goals. Traditionally, we just worked until we set up home and hearth and began knitting booties. Therefore, if you really don't know how to establish your goals, find a workshop that deals with this subject. Or read the book *What Color Is Your Parachute?* by Richard Bolles, which is helpful in establishing professional goals. Your first step should be to take steps to learn how to establish goals.

EXERCISING GOOD JUDGMENT

Do you exercise every day, or is your calendar much too full to fit in an hour of swimming or racquetball? If you are too busy to exercise, you are probably too busy and need to reorder your priorities. Finding time to stretch your muscles means you are exercising good time management. If you are sickly or tire easily, you won't be working up to your full potential.

Now that you've sized things up, you might consider stopping by your health spa after work instead of drinking; as an alternative, you can be a good sport during lunch by playing tennis, running around, or taking a hike.

Remember that Running an Office Is No Different from Running a Home Except Running an Office Is Easier

When you are plotting your strategy for squeezing more time out of your day at the office, don't discount the basic training you learned as a wife and mother and volunteer. Most women have been performing brilliant juggling acts for years in one of the most difficult executive positions there is: homemaker! Don't minimize the skills you learned in this important role. Any woman who has mastered the split-second timing of feeding a cranky baby while carpooling a hoard of rowdy kids and preparing a report for The League of Women Voters is a paragon of organization. Transfer these important assets to the business world and you will be ahead of the game. Men may have had many advantages in the executive arena, but we women are eons ahead in terms of the valuable organizational skills learned on the home front.

Carol Price feels women sometimes make better executives because they are such expert time jugglers. "As a homemaker, a woman learns to jump from one thing to another. This can work well for the woman executive who has to skip from one phone call to another and switch subjects with lightning speed while being constantly interrupted by people who need her counsel."

Keep in mind that the office should seem like a piece of cake compared with being at home. Dr. Estelle Ramey notes that "being at work is much easier than being at home. Problems at home are never solved. When I come into my office, I get respect from secretaries, students, etc. At home no one pays much attention to me. That's why men like to come to the office. Why the hell would they want to stay home?"

Entertaining

Entertaining is one of the most time-consuming things there is. It is sometimes almost impossible for the businesswoman to find time to fit it into her busy schedule. One woman I interviewed confessed, "I kept thinking that one day things would settle down and I would have gorgeous dinner parties—the type you always see in the magazines. Finally, I decided I was only kidding myself—that with my life-style, that day would never come!"

So don't torture yourself and make yourself feel guilty because you are not the Perle Mesta of your block. Entertaining takes time and money—both of which are in scarce supply today.

Remember that old but true maxim—people are coming to see you, not to inspect your bathroom or critique your food, and you don't need to sterilize every square inch of the house and serve rare gourmet delicacies.

If you want to entertain, however, here are some tips on how to keep it simple:

1. Have pot lucks. They are informal and fun and keep you from doing all the work.

2. Suggest a progressive party—drinks at one house, main course at the next, dessert at the last. This can be great fun and not too much work for any one person.

3. Have a wine tasting—ask each guest to bring a favorite bottle of wine. You provide the cheese and bread and it will be an easy and inexpensive evening.

4. Consider asking people over for drinks and appetizers, then going out together for dinner.

5. Ask people over merely for dessert.

6. Try scheduling two evenings in a row for entertaining so that house cleaning and other preparations will serve two purposes.

7. Schedule evenings with friends and social obligations in bunches—do it all in one week, keep the next week free.

Shirley Conran has several tips on how to acquire an "instant gourmet reputation":

"Don't try to compete, don't try to do what good cooks with the necessary time can. Instead, do what even they can rarely find time for. I make my own bread, my own yogurt, [and so forth] . . ."

Conran on coffee: "I grind my coffee beans fresh in a little electric grinder. I get away with culinary murder. If you want to establish a reputation as a gourmet cook, just do this and practically nothing else.

"Make certain when you entertain that you get everyone in on the act. If you are cooking a whole dinner, ask your husband if he wouldn't like to make his special dessert. Get the whole family involved: your kids can help set the table, everyone can help clean up, two of you can divide and conquer at the grocery."[7]

If you make the preparation a group activity, entertaining can be fun. If, on the other hand, you are doing everything yourself, you will probably resent it and will wish all those people would stay home!

"Our life is frittered away by detail . . . simplify, simplify."

Thoreau

It is no brilliant revelation on my part to point out that most of us lead lives fraught with "hecticity." We take on more than we should, frantically rush around, and to what avail? A distressing part of the way in which businesswomen are gaining equality with men is that women are suffering more heart attacks, ulcers, and anxiety attacks. They are becoming nervous wrecks like many male executives. Certainly this is not the type of equality we are striving for!

Heed Thoreau's advice and "Simplify." You don't have to retreat to the woods and subsist on nuts and berries, but you can make your life more tranquil by not obligating yourself to things you don't want to do.

BE CAREFUL OF BEING OVERLY ORGANIZED

I love schemes and formulas that make things easier. I spend half my time coming up with definitive plans on how to save time, and sometimes I've wasted more time on my innovative time-saving devices than if I had just gone ahead and done the job. As a result, I've learned from experience that it is sometimes more efficient to jump in and tackle a job than to try to outsmart it.

You also have to be careful that you are not so organized that your life is as rigid as the stereotype German industrialist who, after working for sixteen hours, announces to his subordinates that it is now time for recreation. He commands, "You will have fun, and you will like it!"

As Sally Richardson, subsidiary rights director for St. Martin's Press, points out, "You need to have time to have fun, too. You don't want to be organized just to be organized. You want to be able to say, 'Screw everything—let's go to the movies right now,' and not have your whole life behind because of that."

So keep in mind that while "Time is of the essence," don't let your fanaticism for perfect timing keep you from having a Good Time.

7

You Work. He Works. But Who Does the Housework?

SURVIVAL TIPS FOR THE DUAL-CAREER COUPLE

> "We are not going to abolish the family. We are not going to abolish marriage. We are not going to abolish the office. But we can change the structure."
>
> *Betty Friedan*
> THE SECOND STAGE

It was a scene I'll never forget. I was in the midst of a presentation with a potential and very influential client. I was trying to convince this distinguished man of the brilliance of my new advertising campaign while at the same time being, if I do say so myself, just the right combination of witty, profound, and earnest. But, just as I was preparing for the grand finale of the presentation, my secretary informed me that I had an emergency phone call.

As I nonchalantly picked up the phone, thoughts flashed through my mind as to who it might be. My client would certainly be impressed if this were the long-awaited phone call telling me that our agency had won first prize in a prestigious advertising show. Unfortunately, it was nothing so positive; it was, instead, a kindergarten teacher who anxiously informed me that my four-year-old daughter had fallen off the swings, onto her head, and that she was now at the emergency room getting stitches.

With one fell swoop, my suave executive image vanished; the polished advertising executive was quickly reduced to a frantic mother who barely said a polite goodbye before dashing off to the hospital. My daughter survived nicely with just a little scar on her forehead.

I'm sorry to say, however, that the potential client remained so. It seems that my daughter's descent made me fall precipitiously from his good graces. I don't think he liked the image of a sophisticated advertising executive turning into an anxious mother before his very eyes. Furthermore, he didn't seem to feel I had my personal life very well in order because I had allowed my daughter to have an accident during working hours.

This may be a severe, but not atypical, example of how working mothers' personal lives can interfere with their careers. You can probably think of myriad others. Since these family distractions are certain to be an inevitable part of your hectic day, have you prepared for them? Do you have a plan of action for the morning when you are expected at an important business meeting and your eight-month-old son becomes ill? Your husband, needless to say, will be out of town on a business trip, your babysitter will call in sick, and you, my dear, will have a crisis on your hands that could affect your career.

Time is always an enormous problem for any working woman. Add a husband and a few children and you need a thirty-hour day. You find yourself wishing that cloning had become a perfected art, especially tonight, when you are expected at an important dinner given by your husband's firm. Your spouse has explained that your presence is very important to him and that, in his rather stodgy firm, wives are expected to attend social functions with their husbands. Just this morning your boss has informed you that *he* expects you to entertain some important clients tonight who have just flown into town. What's a woman to do?

Or what if you have a good four hours' work to catch up on this evening and both you and your husband are too exhausted to fix dinner? And don't forget that one of you promised to go watch your eight-year-old twins portraying chipmunks in their school play tonight. To make matters worse, the washing machine is on the fritz, which means you'll be appearing at that crucial early morning meeting with ring around the collar.

In a different scenario, let's assume that your job calls for entertaining in your home. On the appointed day of the gala soiree, you are all set. Thoughts of how impressed your clients will be with your cozy home and hearth and your spectacular cooking dance happily in your head. Unexpectedly, the phone rings and your cleaning lady reports that she can't come in today because her infected hangnail is acting up. Before you have recovered from this, your daughter calls to inform you that since the Little League game is rained out, the team will be coming over after school to practice in your living room. Your housekeeper reports in to say that she has been exposed to German measles. And your husband has just come home with the flu. You quickly wonder if your clients might opt for some Kentucky Fried Chicken, say, in Kentucky!

What to Do When You Both Need a Wife

Ah! The Dual-Career Marriage. It sounds so appealing! A bright, highly motivated woman arrives home to her equally stimulating and dedicated husband. *Time* magazine calls this duo the "new elite" and announces that for them "the good life has arrived early." According to this optimistic tale, we married workers have more buying power than our parents did at our age. We spend more than single-income families on entertainment, furniture, foods and wines, restaurant meals, and, especially, on exotic travel. We, in other words, have it made.

What a life! The sweet smell of success, the double roar of achievement. Two high-powered careers, 2.5 adorable children, and two elevated paychecks that add up to one contemporary storybook marriage. Everything you could ever want! The only rub is that this lovely dual-career marriage myth is a fairy tale just like *Cinderella*. The reality is that a dual-career marriage is filled with problems which threaten both marriage and career.

Dual-career couples, it seems, are flocking to marriage counselors in droves; the therapists report that a two-career marriage is one of the most difficult life-styles a couple can ever choose. Both the divorce rate and the mortality toll on careers are extremely high in dual-career marriages, and why? Well, for one thing, we have no good role models to emulate since most of us were raised in traditional families. We are essentially modern pioneers exploring a new frontier. It can be exciting to be part of this pilgrim's progress, but the casualty rate will be extremely high!

HOME ON THE RANGE—PROBLEMS ON THE NEW FRONTIER

If you both have high-powered careers, chances are you'll also have some high-powered problems. First among these might be the dilemma of whose career takes precedence. Suppose, for instance, that you are duly recognized as the illustrious vice-president of a major Chicago brokerage firm. Your husband, a biochemist, is offered the presidency of a small Vermont college. What to do? Do you pull up stakes and dutifully follow him in the hope that you might find a decent job somewhere along the line? Or do you opt for career over marriage? As an alternative might you eventually try a commuting marriage?

What about children? To have or not to have? If you do choose to have them, will your husband take paternity leave? Will you interrupt your important career? Or will you choose some sort of child care? Who will have psychological responsibility for this child? Who will stay home with him when he is sick? Who will hire the babysitter and check in with her every day?

How about the exhaustion factor? If you are both channeling much of your energy into your respective careers, will there be any left for your relationship? Many dual-career couples report that they are too tired most evenings to sustain the energy for sex. On the flip side, if you do channel a great deal of your energy into your home and family, will there be enough left over for your career?

With the heavy demands imposed by two careers, will there be time for social life? What about a quiet moment for you to be alone? This may be a true luxury, if not an impossibility, for a working wife and mother.

Who controls the money and who pays for what? Can you avoid the pitfall of thinking that what he earns is ours, and what you earn is yours?

Can you really have it all—career, husband, and kids—or is that some new myth that is being forced down our throats? Are you still trying to be Superwoman by proving that you can be the perfect wife, mother, and career woman? If you are, forget it. As Shirley Conran points out: "Realize that you can't do everything. Don't believe a word you read about those ladies in the glossy magazines who seem to be so perfect. They're either outright liars or they're ruthlessly selfish, giving their families hell and having a little light, nervous, noisy breakdown every third month."[1]

HOW TO SURVIVE AND EVEN THRIVE

This chapter will not try to be all things to all people. The subject of Dual-Career Marriages is enormously complex, and entire books have been devoted to it. Rather than musing over the philosophical problems and general difficulties, let's consider specific tips on how to make your life easier. This section will offer pertinent advice on how to run your home and career smoothly with the least amount of stress. Here you will learn how best to get resource people, how to pick a day-care center for your child, how to stop being the maid in your own home, and how to get your family to pitch in.

So, if your dual-career marriage is making you feel like you are in a career "duel" rather than being part of a dynamic duo, this chapter is for you!

"A LITTLE DIRT NEVER HURT ANYONE," OR "HOW TO LOWER YOUR STANDARDS"

Hey you! Stop trying to be perfect! Do you think that years from now anyone will remember whether your dinners were awarded four stars from Michelin, or if your home looked as if *House and Garden* were coming over to do a full-page color spread? What your family and your co-workers will more likely remember is what a grouch you were while you were wearing yourself to a frazzle. So relax and stop trying to live up to absurd and unrealistic standards.

As Gene Barnes advises, "A working woman must learn to live with a certain amount of confusion and lack of organization. If you are going to let it bother you, then you have to make a choice. Either you have to give up work and take care of your house or be willing to settle for what you are able to do."

Some things are worth doing poorly. The first step in learning how not to be perfect is to realize that your house doesn't have to be constantly prepared to pass a white-glove inspection. Unless Queen Elizabeth drops over regularly and unannounced for tea, you might consider relaxing your standards a bit. I have adopted a comforting albeit scientific thought that gets me through many a harrowing day when beds aren't made and my house looks as if it had just been invaded by two hundred two-year-olds at a rowdy birthday party. Acccording to my husband, the physicist (and he ought to know), being neat and tidy is an exercise in futility. Being the Felix Unger of your block merely defies the laws of the universe since the natural order of the universe is disorder! Cleaning up, in other words, is actually an act of defiance. Look at it this way. Every time you make that bed and dust that coffee table, you are messing around with the Laws of Thermodynamics. Cleanliness is next to sacrilege, and Einstein wouldn't have liked it.

If my lovely rationalization of carrying logic to its irrational conclusion doesn't make you put down that broom, consider this. If Ernest Hemingway had taken time to clean out his refrigerator, the world might never have had *The Sun Also Rises.* Imagine what Leonardo da Vinci might not have invented had he stopped to clean out his closet!

Develop a sense of humor about never-finished chores. Would you rather be remembered as someone who never had waxy buildup on her floors than as a competent professional and a loving wife and mother?

Help! How to Put Your Money Where Your Time is

Being a martyr went out with Joan of Arc, so stop trying to do everything yourself. There is too much at stake. Admit to yourself that you can't do it all, and that you're not Wonder Woman. Even if you can physically tackle everything, think of what it is costing you in terms of emotional wear and tear and strained family relations.

Conran suggests: "Figure out how you can get other people to do the things you hate, but can't eliminate, and work out how much it would cost you in terms of money and spirit. Develop the fine art of farming things out."

If money is no object.   If you can afford it, the best solution is full-time, live-in household help. Most of the high-powered women I interviewed agreed that having a staff of modern-day Mary Poppins in their homes was the only way they could survive. Although these women had in-house staffs that ran the gamut from housekeeper, governess, and cook to a combination of all of these, all agreed upon one thing—you must be willing to pay extremely well. As Amy Greene, who has had a housekeeper for many years, puts it, "You should get the best help that money can buy!"

Having full-time help won't necessarily turn your life into a rerun of "Father Knows Best" but, as Dr. Estelle Ramey observes, "It will reduce the pain." Years ago when Ramey was a bride, she was smart enough to "buy a housewife for myself" so she could pursue her career and simultaneously raise two children.

Help for the more plebeian.   Some of us, alas, are condemned to live servantless lives. For us, a nanny is just a storybook figure from long-ago bedtime tales. The closest we have come to a live-in is when our ten-year-old's best friend stays overnight. So what choices, other than running away from home, do those of us with more modest means have? Do not be the one to worry, because help is at hand.

Today's answer to The White Knight—the cleaning person.   For most of us working women, the biggest aid to running a home is probably the cleaning person. If you hire someone to come in at least once a week, you immediately eliminate the inevitable marital discussions and sometimes even fisticuffs about whose turn it is to clean the bathroom.

Having your cleaning person quit is dirty business. Quickly the rest of your life becomes very "dish-oriented." Sally Richardson found this out when "the wonderful woman who we had for five years got sick and it took me about three months to find someone who was good. I thought I would go nuts. It was so disorganized having a dirty house, and I just got so depressed. It meant cleaning the house on the weekend, scrubbing the floors, or it meant not entertaining the way we did. It's amazing how much that screwed up my life. I was a wreck. I didn't have any fun for a couple of months. And you can't do your job when you're unhappy. If you're worried about something like that outside, you can't function right."

Be resourceful about how you find your household resource people. In big cities there are, of course, agencies that specialize in domestic help of all types. However, when you get out into the provinces, you have to be a bit more inventive. Santa Fe, where I live, is an exceptional case. In Santa Fe there are no conventional cleaning services. There are also essentially no sources of what I would call "real jobs." Therefore, one finds terribly overqualified people doing rather menial work, just for the privilege of living in what they consider nirvana. My present cleaning lady, as an example, is a graduate of Rutgers University, a former dancer with Merce Cunningham, and an excellent artist. She has found that this part-time job pays her more than anything else in this low-income town. It has wonderful fringe benefits for me as well. After all, how many people can discuss a current show at the Metropolitan Museum, the perfect recipe for matzo ball soup, and the latest scuttlebutt on the local art scene—with their cleaning lady? The pièce de résistance is that she is also a wonderful cleaner.

The student prince.   Sometimes finding resource people requires giving it the old college try. Marlene Sanders at one time "had a student live-in from the local university whose duties were dinner, dishes, and baby-sitting." Marie Hirst has found that "if you are near a college or a university, there are resource people by the dozens—a real wide variety of talent. Students always need money, and if you travel a lot you can get students to stay and take care of your pets and water your plants. Students always have offbeat talents. For instance, I have a girl who comes to our house every day; she is a fantastic ironer and she loves straightening closets. It's like having a lady's maid."

The ever-resourceful Hirst suggests that another overlooked possibility is the trusty Eagle Scout. "Eagle Scouts know how to do everything, and Eagle Scouts are always looking for ways to earn money, because they are taught to be useful citizens. If you have an Eagle Scout in the neighborhood, he'll walk your dog, chop your wood, etc."

Like a good scout, "be prepared."   Don't wait till you have a crisis on your hands to find resource people to help you out. Sally Richardson finds that advance planning in her busy life is crucial: "Make friends with your butcher, your wine store, and places like that. It's amazing how they can help you out. I mean if you said you were coming to dinner now, I could call the butcher and say, 'Would you deliver such and such?' and it would be there. Since these things are so important, it's worth the time to get them set up. It's worth spending a Saturday going around and introducing yourself and opening an account."

The Politics of Housework

Don't—I repeat *don't*—be the maid in your own home. Even if you have a once-a-week cleaning person, you're going to need some help with the daily humdrum chores. So forget this nonsense about being a slave to your family. That type of housewifely masochism went out in the sixties about the time Betty Friedan was making us aware of the feminine mystique.

You may think housework is unimportant, hardly worth turning into a major family issue. However, according to Letty Cottin Pogrebin, housework is a very political issue: "Housework is physical and mental, personal and political. . . . Both doing and remembering housework take one away from other things, therefore housework is not trivial; it steals one's life."[2]

WHERE IS THAT "NEW MAN" WE'VE BEEN HEARING ABOUT?

There has been a lot of lip service paid to the new breed of male helpmate that exists today. It is not all science fiction, I am happy to report, since I am indeed married to one such liberated man. David and I, during our fourteen-year marriage, have split all household chores, including child-rearing, right down the middle. As a matter of fact, since I have been working on this book, he has assumed the lion's share of our household's smooth functioning. Most nights he cooks, as well as does the dishes (after doing the marketing). It is conceivable, I suppose, that he is doing all this so that I will write these kind words about him, but that seems a heavy price to pay for a few sentences of purple prose.

At the same time, however, I was unhappy to find that he is the exception rather than the rule. Most husbands of working wives remain the Archie Bunkers of their castles.

Letty Cottin Pogrebin explains that most husbands and housework are incompatible and that housework is often a power struggle: "In two-adult homes, the way housework time is allocated tells us something important about who exercises power—power over free time and labor, if nothing else. Here's what the studies show:

". . . Women who are employed spend just under five hours [per day] on house and family work.

"Men spend about an hour and a half a day on house and family work whether their wives are homemakers or employed. . . .

"In other words, on the average wives do 70 percent of the housework while husbands and children each do 15 percent."

Are men totally to blame for these alarming statistics? You can bet your dishpan hands that they aren't!

Women often don't ask for help; instead, they somehow feel that household chores are their responsibility; upbringing dies hard, it seems. Pogrebin attempts to explain this unfortunate syndrome which seems to be doing women in. "Sex role strain is alive and well because so many women are still overdosing on the feminine mystique, still confusing their personal identity with a clean house, still fearing male disapproval and doing penance for stepping out of the domestic sphere. For all her new earning power, the nontraditional woman remains trapped by tradition."[3]

In other words, we working women still seem to be winning top honors in the Guilt Sweepstakes. Take the case of Diane Stevens, a gifted biochemist who does almost all the housework in addition to her taxing work load.

"I guess I feel guilty asking for help. Even though it sounds so old-fashioned, I still somehow feel that the housework should be my responsibility."

Marjorie Levine, a Cleveland executive with AT&T, observes in the book, *Views from Women Achievers*, that "A career woman who gives any indication that she's more absorbed in her work than in her husband and her family is neither understood nor forgiven very easily. . . . So women find themselves trying to make sure that they do all the things that women are traditionally supposed to do, on top of all their work responsibilities. We're often not too comfortable with delegating household tasks. I have that attitude myself. . . . I do most of my own housework, and I find myself entertaining a good deal, deliberately preparing every morsel of food. And doing it without help."

What is behind Levine's Superwoman-type zeal? "I know that my motivation is to communicate to everybody—to my husband and all the friends who think that he is not really getting a fair shake out of all this work and travel and so forth—to convince them that I'm really a woman and I'm really not letting down that end of the bargain."[4]

My advice on this subject is to leave Guilt (with a capital G) to old-style Jewish mothers who thrive on it. For, if you don't, this Superwoman complex will do you in. Save the important energy for your career and your family and stop being a martyr. This self-sacrificing image is terrible for you and serves as a rotten example for working women everywhere.

And, now that you are going to work on guilt-free living, how, you may ask, are you going to find the help you need? Fortunately for you, rhetorical questions usually beget simple answers, and all you have to do is read on.

The Psychology of Housework

"There is only one way two working people, with assorted children, a large dog, two cats, and two guinea pigs, can make a home more than a hovel and less than a prison, and that's by a division of labor according to each's inclination and fancy."   *Anne Roiphe*

Marriages used to fall apart over such things as Mental Cruelty and Adultery. A modern dual-career marriage is more likely to break up over Housework. If you and your spouse are continually fighting over the Dust Bowl (i.e., whose turn it is to dust and generally clean up) or if you are tackling all the work yourself while your husband lounges around waiting for dinner to be served, here are some tips that could save both your marriage and your career:

Don't suffer in silence.   Most husbands aren't clairvoyant or for that matter even very observant. Therefore, if you are silently glaring or moaning and groaning with an occasional sigh thrown in, your husband may think you merely have the flu or are in training for a nonassertiveness class.

So, be direct! Tell your husband that you need help around the house. If you don't, you have no one to blame but yourself.

Treat the problem as a management situation rather than a marital crisis.   Make an appointment with your spouse to discuss dividing household responsibilities. Let's face it—the professional approach certainly beats trying to blurt out your sentiments during a thirty-second commercial while your gross husband is engrossed in the Sunday NFL double-header.

Get out of the house to discuss home sweet home.   You may find it useful to be away from the house (and children) for that first talk. There shouldn't be many interruptions, and people are more likely to be calm and reasonable in a restaurant than at home.

One other tip on making this first meeting run smoothly: don't be accusatory and don't dredge up ancient wounds. This is *not* the moment to mention, for the thousandth time, that you thought it was a little tacky for his mother to have worn black to the wedding, or that you don't feel that season tickets to the Knicks games was an appropriate seventh anniversary present (even with a year's supply of popcorn thrown in). Stick to the subject at hand.

CLEANLINESS IS NEXT TO IMPOSSIBLE, BUT . . .

When you have finally made it clear to your husband that you're tired of being the maid in your own home, what then?

List all household chores. Some men have no earthly idea how a household functions. They think that toilet paper grows magically in the bathrooms and that the food in the pantry breeds overnight and hence replenishes itself. It may be that your husband will be amazed when gazing upon your mile-long list to realize how many things must be done to keep the house running marginally, let alone smoothly.

"Odds bodkins," your startled spouse may expound, "I had no idea that you did all these things to keep home and hearth together." Sometimes the very list can provide the incentive that will change a man's attitude.

KP time. Once those around you have ceased being listless, there are several possible approaches as to the best way to press them into service. One of the following methods should serve your purposes:

1. Make independent judgments. Both of you, and children, too, should go through the list and make independent decisions about each one's availability for specific tasks, noting his and her skills in performing it. This method works best when one of you insists upon being the Tidy Bowl man while the other demands the privilege of getting your clothes "whiter than white." It's when you both independently decide you want to cook and begin fighting over who *gets* to do the dishes that the problem starts. If this is the case, you might consider the following option.

2. Rotating the duties. Suppose you and your spouse both fancy yourselves as galloping gourmets, but look forward to tackling those dishes with the same relish you would reserve for enlisting in World War III. The only sensible solution is to take turns.

3. Become a pointillist. If your family members are sticklers for fairness, consider a scheme which should get the point across.

Have everyone make a list (including every chore necessary for survival) and assign each task a point value based either on how many hours it takes or how onerous it is. Divide the chores so each family member gets the same number of points. It will all add up to a smooth division of labor.

4. Decide which chores are most important to each person and divide them accordingly.   If your husband can't sleep at night because the floors aren't waxed, then let him wax them. On the other hand, if you get upset if your boa constrictor's cage isn't spotlessly clean, then you should be the one to clean it.

5. Divide chores according to your natural skills.   If your husband's culinary skills would put Craig Claiborne to shame and you are the greatest car mechanic this side of Janet Guthrie, then it's obvious how to divide your chores.

Bear in mind that you and your husband should be willing to teach each other. Many women, by virtue of an entire lifetime of training, forget that skills are indeed required for many jobs. Making an apple cobbler certainly isn't as easy as pie on the first few tries. Likewise, fixing the plumbing can be a wrenching experience without the needed training.

6. What's mine is yours—splitting the chores right down the middle.   Here's how this 50-50 plan works: I'll chop up the Chinese vegetables, if you'll stir-fry them. We'll divide and conquer at the grocery. I'll get tomatoes, you'll get potatoes. Get the idea?

You could divide the work week in half or alternate chores on an every-other-day basis. You might even throw darts at a dart board filled with chores and decide that way. Be inventive. Maybe housework will even start to be fun.

THE MOST IMPORTANT CHORE OF ALL IS PSYCHOLOGICAL
RESPONSIBILITY

What is psychological responsibility? Do you have it? Is it contagious? Can you get it by kissing on the first date?

Actually, psychological responsibility means that one of you is *totally* in charge of a particular task, the thinking about it, remembering it, and carrying it out. For instance, say that your husband has psychological responsibility for the laundry and taking Susi to her Little League every week. If he doesn't do these things, they simply don't get done. In other words, you don't have to keep reminding him; he's not merely helping you out. *It is his job.*

Merily Keller, an Austin public relations specialist, feels that "there's a difference between sharing the work and having the psychological responsibility. With a child, for example, there always has to be one person who takes the psychological responsibility, one person, in other words, who knows all the petty details—like what shoes he wears, when he's a new baby, what new foods to introduce."

Carol Price claims that the fact that her husband, George, started taking psychological responsibility for part of the household kept their marriage and her career going.

She explains that "the thinking about what there is to do is where it all lies. A long time ago I had to explain to George (and to myself) that it didn't work for him just to be helpful. He had to take full responsibility for certain areas of work that were just his and that I didn't have to worry about."

Remembrance of things past.   Maybe your husband can remember the Alamo and recall the Maine but seems to forget everybody's birthdays. You, on the other hand, are a repository for such data. You can always be relied on to recount every family event, including the anniversary of the day your gerbils escaped from their cage. You shop for all the presents, and write every thank-you note, for which, in your large family, is indeed an arduous task.

If this tale of "Forgetfulness of Things Past" is not a novel event in your household, then the only sensible solution is to count the act of remembering as labor and exchange it for other household work. Here's how this works: I'll remember to make the grocery list, you do the shopping; I remember all the birthdays; you buy the presents and cards.

CHARITY BEGINS AT HOME

If you husband or children take over their share of the housework, *don't complain* if their work doesn't meet your high standards. At least they are doing something. In other words, if you entrust them with a job, don't be a buttinski. Let them do the chore the way they see fit. If it doesn't meet your high standards, leave the room or get out of the house.

A friend of mine, a record company executive whom I shall call

Sara T., griped incessantly that her husband never helped with the housework. Then, when he started helping, she griped even more. When he did the grocery shopping, she chided him for spending too much money and getting wilted lettuce. When he tried his hand at the laundry, she complained because the clothes always looked gray and weren't folded just the way she liked them.

Finally, the inevitable happened. Her husband exploded, "You yell like hell if I don't do my fair share, but my share is never good enough. If you want things done your way, then do them yourself!"

After he stormed out, Sara realized that she had been coming across like a Goody Two-Shoes housewife straight out of a laundry commercial. From then on, she shut up and stopped playing the Grand Inquisitor when her spouse did his househusbandly chores. Things weren't done as perfectly as she would have done them, but at least they were done.

Some More of Peggy Elaine's Household Hints

1. What to do if you're a Felix Unger type married to an Oscar Madison. If your husband was raised in a household that was always immaculate and you were brought up in a home where the beds were made only once a year when your grandmother visited, then you could be at odds over standards of cleanliness.

The most expedient solution, outside of divorce or homicide, is compromise. The Oscar Madison of your couple should make a concerted effort to be tidier, while the Felix Unger learns to button his lip and overlook a few things.

A preventative, rather than a remedy, is to consider marriage only to someone who shares your views on housework. Lois Sherman, a Voice of America writer, finds that "it helps if you have a similar attitude about housework." Fortunately, she and her husband John, a teacher, see eye to eye (or dust to dust) on this subject, and hence "keep minimum house. We never make the beds," Lois says laughingly, "and the living room floor gets vacuumed only when somebody is coming over."

2. Peggy's Do-It-Themselves Plan. You're really doing your children and yourself a disservice if you perform tasks for them that they could do for themselves. They will grow up overprivileged, and you will grow old fast. My children started doing their own chores at age seven. Lisa, when she was eleven, was turning out prize-winning croissants and brioches and helping plan meals. If I had done all these chores for my kids, I would have been too exhausted to do my job, and they would never have learned any household skills.

2. *Eliminate clutter.*   Remember—the less you have, the less you have to keep clean. Go through your home and eliminate every item you don't need, like the broken chair nobody ever sits in, the ashtrays that haven't been used since you quit smoking, and that pile of yellowing newspapers that you're "going to get to someday."

To help you decide what to throw away, consider taking some pictures. The mess you've grown oblivious to may look like pure unadulterated clutter in a photograph.

4. *Some don'ts on time-consuming things.*

Don't make the beds—use comforters instead.

Don't buy anything that needs ironing.

Don't dry dishes.

Don't cook a deluxe hot meal every night—if your budget allows it, eat out several nights. Or some evenings just make sandwiches. We all eat too much, anyway!

5. *Try to evolve your own basic life-style.*   Heed the sage words from Shirley Conran, who advises, "Aim for one [a life-style] that allows for the fact that you can't get a quart out of a pint jar, and that focuses on your own capacities and limitations, not someone else's set of oughts and shoulds."[5]

6. *Focus your energy where you are.*   If you spend most of your time at work worrying about Johnny's sore throat or tonight's dinner, you will probably be a lousy worker and might as well have stayed home. Likewise, at home, if you are totally preoccupied with job-related problems, you won't be an effective wife and mother. So draw a mental line of demarcation between home and office and give your full energies to whichever place you happen to be.

A Delicate Balance—The Juggling Act of Working Mothers

"The combination of motherhood with a career can send even the calmest of us screaming for help, as we treat a child's skinned knee with one hand while massaging a client's ego with the other. How to cope? With firmly established priorities and a good sense of humor."   *Linda Bird Francke*

There must be a special place in heaven for working mothers—a quiet corner where there are no lunch boxes to pack, no 3 P.M. parent-teacher conference to try to fit in, and no anxiety attacks about whether your child is receiving tender love and care while you are working.

Since heaven can wait, let's get back to earth and figure out some practical solutions to the most common problems that working mothers face. To begin with the most vexing dilemma, what to do with your child while you work, let's look at various options to see which one is best for you.

And baby makes three.   Perhaps the most difficult decision is figuring out what to do with a child under three years of age. Many working mothers, especially those who have a baby when they are older and their career is established, are amazed at how difficult it is to leave an infant. Parting from your child, of course, will be much less traumatic if you feel that your baby has the best possible care. Here are some choices for helping hands:

1. The full-time governess.   Having a nanny is, of course, the best of all possible worlds. With a live-in Mary Poppins, your life should be supercalifragilisticexpialidocious.

2. The nine-to-five caregiver who comes to your house.   This arrangement has lots of advantages since you can hand-pick the person who cares for your child. You won't have to take the baby out of the house on cold, dark mornings or when she's sick. More importantly, your baby will have one person other than her parents who understands and cares for her.

3. Care by relatives.   The primary advantage to this relatively simple agreement is so elementary that even John Watson might have been able to figure it out. A major benefit is that you should certainly know what you are getting. The major disadvantage, which might not be so obvious, is that, when the baby turns into a toddler (as she inevitably will), a grandmother may not have enough physical energy to keep up with her.

4. Family day care.   A family day care simply means that your child is taken care of by a man or woman who has a family. Many of the mothers that I interviewed felt that such a family day care, when well done, was a much warmer and more stimulating experience for a very young child than the best day-care group center. And why? Because it offers a real home environment with real food cooking on the stove and real telephones ringing. In other words, it is about as close to being at home as your child can get. Also, since your child is actually in someone's home, she is learning basic concepts about essential things instead of being in a make-believe playhouse.

Some questions to ask when checking out a family day care include:

a. Is it licensed?
b. Is the home close to where you work or live?
c. Is the person in charge young enough to have the necessary energy, yet old enough to be experienced?
d. Is the house neat and clean without being too prissy and intimidating for a young child?
e. Will it be well-ventilated in the summer and well-heated in the winter?
f. Does it have a fenced yard for safe outdoor play?
g. Do they serve nutritious meals?
h. Do they offer educational activities that are to your liking?
i. What are your gut-level feelings as to whether: the day-care person really likes children, has a sense of humor, is a person you feel happy leaving your children with?

IT'S 10 O'CLOCK. DO YOU KNOW WHERE YOUR CHILDREN ARE?

What type of child care is best for children in the two- to six-year-old age group? All of the ones mentioned above are, of course, applicable. Perhaps the most popular facility for older children is the group day-care center. Let's look at its advantages and disadvantages:

Advantages.

1. Day cares come under government regulation, and while you may not be certain of the best care, they are required to meet established standards of child care.

2. The center staffs have higher degrees of professionalism than other kinds of care. In particular, the directors should have degrees in early childhood education.

3. Your children will be constantly supervised.

4. Day cares are dependable; they are always open and there is always someone to care for the child.

5. Day care provides continuity of place and routine.

Disadvantages.

1. The loss of a one-to-one relationship.

2. Expense, since day cares are usually the most expensive of all choices.

HOW TO CHOOSE A GOOD DAY-CARE CENTER

Suppose you decide that your child would be happiest in a good day-care center, but you wouldn't recognize a good one when you see it? I suggest that you look for the following:

1. An accommodating administrator who sets up meetings for your convenience rather than hers.

2. A good adult/child ratio—no more than three infants or ten older children to one adult.

3. A curriculum that is responsive to your child's needs.

4. Nurturing care-givers instead of TV sets.

5. Flexibility—can you pick your child up early or leave her late?

6. Teachers who are aware of "end of the day" problems (i.e., who realize that both parents and children are tired and often irritable). Teachers, therefore, should have all the child's materials packed and ready to go when the parent arrives.

7. A nonsexist place where boys can play with dolls and girls can build bridges.

You'll want to visit the day-care center several times and carefully observe it at various times of the day. Here are some tips to keep in mind while forming your impression:

Make your first visit unannounced so you can see what the center is really like rather than what they want you to think it is like.

Take a notebook listing the major questions to ask the director—don't forget to make notes during the visit.

Go once during lunch to see what type of food your child will be served.

Look around you and observe if there is a safe outside play area and if the classrooms are large enough to accommodate separate play areas.

On the second or third visit, bring your child with you. Watch carefully how the staff treats her. If they ignore her or seem annoyed when she interrupts, then this isn't the place for you.

Call some parents of children who attend the center, and see if they are satisfied.

If you are still baffled by the confusing world of day cares, there are several places where you can go for advice, including:

The local chapter of the National Association for Education of Young Children.

The social service department of the local hospital.

A teaching college or university that has a child-study program.

Your church, synagogue, or local family service organization.

For more general information you might consider sending for the following publications:

"How to Choose," available from the National Association for the Education of Young Children, 1834 Connecticut Avenue, NW, Washington, DC 20009.

"How to Select Child Day Care," "How to Select Family Day Care," the two are also combined in a Spanish version, from Child Care Resource Center, 24 Thorndike Street, Cambridge, MA 02141.

You might also want to invest in the excellent book, *Ourselves and Our Children*, by the Boston Women's Health Book Collective (New York: Random House, 1978).

MORE PRACTICAL TIPS ON CHILD CARE

1. The fail-safe contingency plan.   If you haven't made provisions for inevitable emergencies, you may eventually find yourself in a peck of trouble. Heed the sage words of Merily Keller who has found that "you need to have a back-up babysitter and a back-up for your back-up. You really should arrange your back-up in advance because otherwise you're going to have a meeting one morning, your husband's going to have a meeting, and the babysitter won't be able to come. Then you've got a real problem."

Keller, a very resourceful mother, certainly practices what she preaches. To insure expert help when her son Sed was sick and she couldn't stay home with him, she called the hospital and got a list of practical baby nurses to hire. "It was a great method. I knew Sed was in good hands so I could go ahead and do my job and not spend the whole day worrying about him."

2. *Consider working near your home or living near your work.*   If your job is an hour's distance or more from your home you may find it difficult, if not downright impossible, to deal with your children's inevitable crises.

3. *Children should be seen and not hurt.*   To ease your mind about your older children's well-being while you're at work, give serious thought to the following recommendations:

Make certain your children have your office telephone number and at least one other number to call in an emergency.

Brief your children on how to call the police and fire departments.

Instruct your children to keep doors locked and not open them to strangers under any circumstances.

Arrange to have a nonworking mother on alert for your child to call should a problem arise.

How to Keep Your Kids from Driving You Crazy

"A suburban mother's role is to deliver children obstetrically once, and by car forever after."   *Peter De Vries*

One of the most time-consuming aspects of having older children involves the almost continual chauffeuring you're called upon to perform. Carpooling and delivering kiddies to various lessons can try the patience of a saint and take up the entire afternoon of a nonworking mother. So how can a working mom possibly be expected to handle this pickup and delivery service? For starters, consider the following:

1. *Try public transportation.*   It can be a good experience in a safe neighborhood for a child to master the city's bus system. This could be the perfect solution for weekly piano or ballet lessons.

2. *Rely on taxi companies.*   For regular pickup and delivery for orthodontists and various lessons and activities.

3. *Call local colleges and universities.*   Inquire at the student employment office for a reliable man or woman who can transport your cherubs around town.

4. Think of your neighbors as a driving force.   Trade their driving time during the week for your driving time at night and on weekends.

5. Check with local social service agencies.   For any retired people who might welcome some extra income and a chance to serve as chauffeuring grandparents to your children.

In any instance where you are relying upon uncertified people, you should, of course, check references and make certain that the drivers have current licenses.

TAKING A TURN FOR THE BETTER

A Chicago friend once told me about an ingenious time-saving plan. A group of working mothers got together and scheduled their children's music lessons, dentist appointments, etc., for the same day of the week and then pooled the driving. As she explained: "About once a month we have a meeting and we each bring our kids' appointment/lesson/paper-route schedules and figure out who can do what."

This concept is a type of co-op that seems to be spreading like inflation throughout the country. There are others that I've heard about, including:

A marketing co-op.   Where women take turns grocery shopping for the group.

An errands collective.   Where women alternate taking care of such details as:

Cleaners—dropping and picking up laundry.

Serving as "the cake mother"—baking all the children's birthday cakes for the month.

Present mother—buying all the birthday presents for the month.

Dropping and picking up library books.

Keeping the shared-sitters list updated.

Scheduling child care for a month at a time.

A "Waiting for the deliveryman" co-op.   One member is on call once a week in the morning. She has everyone's house keys and is around to supervise deliveries and sign the invoices.

Babysitting Co-op.   The perfect solution to free babysitting all year long.

Many of these co-ops have fringe benefits as well. John Sherman in his guide to setting up an easy-care babysitting co-op, explains: "Being in the co-op has given our children a lot more friends they might not have met otherwise; it serves as an extended family for us, and we are all very comfortable with one another. Most of us have no family in our community, so this gives us that 'family'—something both generations welcome."[6]

How the Country is Changing to Accommodate Two-Career Families

What then does the future hold for working couples? What is most desperately needed is a support system offered by corporations and communities. Our system, as it now exists, isn't working because women are still making most of the sacrifices.

Certainly, women today have opportunities as never before, but only if they are willing to give up crucial things or put on their Superwoman cape and risk burnout. Our society does not make it easy for women to succeed without paying a heavy price. As an article entitled "Time Pressured Lives" (*Savvy*, December 1980) puts it: "They [successful women] lead rather austere lives. . . . While opportunities for women have burgeoned, quality of lives has declined. To do what we live best, we have sacrificed many simple pleasures including sleep, privacy, friends, nest-building, pets, home-cooked food and in some cases, children."

Or as Letty Cottin Pogrebin, puts it: "The female sex role imperative has expanded to allow women to 'have it all' as long as they can do it all."

". . . what passes for the new 'liberated' two-career family reveals itself to be a three-career family: The wife does two jobs, paid work and family work, while the husband does one. Thus, the supposed equality signaled by the rising number of employed wives and mothers may actually signal an alarming increase in overworked women."[7]

What is sorely needed is a consciousness-raising effort to get the message across that the corporation and the community must respond to the dual-career family. Innovative ideas must be instituted to better serve the changing work force. Betty Friedan feels that this problem is the new issue facing the women's movement. In her book *The Second Stage*, she explains how our collective attitudes must change: "In the second stage we have to transcend that polarization between feminism and the family. . . . The second stage is not as much a fixed agenda as it is a process,

a mode that will put a new value on qualities once considered—
and denigrated as—special to women, feminine qualities that will
be liberated in men as they share experiences like child care. . . .

"In the second stage, women will have to say 'No' to standards
of success on the job set in terms of men who had wives to take
care of all the details of life, and standards at home set in terms
of women whose whole sense of worth and power had to come
from that perfectly run house, those perfectly controlled children.

"Instead of accepting that double burden, women will realize
that they can and must give up some of that power in the home
and the family when they are carrying part of the breadwinning
burden and some beginnings of power on the job. Instead of those
rigid contracts that seemed the feminist ideal in the first stage,
there will be in the second stage an easy flow as man and woman
share the chores of home and children—sometimes 50-50, sometimes 20-80, or 60-40, according to their abilities and needs.

"Above all," Friedan assures us, "the second stage involves not
a retreat to the family, but embracing the family in new terms of
equality and diversity."[8]

How is this new egalitarianism going to work? Although our
country is certainly not moving at lightning speed as far as helping make the lot of dual-career families easier, some innovations
and encouraging signs are occurring already.

Some may be skeptical about this optimistic outlook, particularly since our country presently seems to be reversing many
hard-won social changes. But in spite of the myriad problems
facing the dual-career family, there is cause for some hope. Here
are some options that can make a dual-career couple's life less
frantic:

Job-sharing.   In job-sharing, two people split the duties of one
job. The "I work in the morning, you work in the afternoon"
concept could be an ideal solution for parents of young children.
It is, in fact, one of the more exciting things to happen in the
work force since someone put white wine in the water cooler.

Flextime.   This approach to flexibility in working hours allows
for a wide range of arrival and departure hours, provided that
everyone is present during the "core time," which is usually in
the middle of the day. The strength of flextime lies in the fact
that giving employees some control over their own schedules gives

them more motivation to work. As a matter of fact, a survey of 805 organizations taken by the American Management Association in 1977 revealed that productivity increased under flextime, absenteeism was 75% lower, and employee morale improved 97 percent.

Working part-time.   Many enlightened companies are allowing employees the opportunity to work only 80 percent of a week. This option was a godsend to Janet Kuhn, an attorney with the Washington D.C. law firm of Steptoe and Johnson. She admitted during our interview that for years she had felt fragmented and torn between her job and her family.

"I never had enough time," she noted. "After a while, I just couldn't handle the strain of being a full-time lawyer, being married, and raising two kids. Now I work only four days a week. This frees me to spend more time with my kids, go to parent-teacher conferences, and actually have a little breathing space for myself."

The compressed work week.   This approach involves working a standard number of hours (thirty-five to forty) in less than the typical five-day work week. One could, for instance, work three long days and take two days off. Melissa Cimabue, a California personnel consultant reports "this method is very popular and effective among single mothers who would rather have a block of quality time to see their kids even if it means working three long hard days."

Split-location jobs.   Using this method, some of your work can be done at home. I am a living example that this system does work, since I do about half my writing and business consulting at home. "Creative piecework," which includes writing, editing, and commercial art, is very compatible with split-location jobs. And it is now sometimes possible to work at home by using computer terminals and closed circuit TV.

At this point you may be wondering if the demand really exists for these kind of innovations. Are people's attitudes changing? Yes. Daniel Yankelovich's book, *New Rules: Searching for Self-fulfillment in a World Turned Upside Down*, reports that there is a substantial change in our attitudes about sex roles, marriage, and family. In 1970 men were asked if "both sexes should share the child-rearing responsibility." At that time 33 percent responded yes. In 1980 it was up to 56 percent. When asked if work was the center of their life, 34 percent said yes in 1970. In 1978 it was down to 13 percent.[9]

In other words, a significant segment of the American male population is responding positively to our needs. These men are changing their value systems. We are seeing a new breed of non-workaholic man who turns down overtime, transfers, and promotions in favor of more time at home and a more stable family life. There are even liberated male executives who balk at travel; they reject late hours and weekend work even when offered double pay. These pioneers have chosen to be more involved with their wives and are playing a major role in rearing their children.

One of the major clogs in the wheel of success, however, is the corporations that employ us. Companies are responding with a remarkable lack of alacrity. Life is still not duck soup for couples who work; the corporate structure is presently not set up for the convenience of dual-career families. However, instances of enlightened changes are taking place, including:

Paternity and maternity leave. Some companies are now offering paternity leave to male workers when their children are born; others are giving longer maternity leave to women. An example that will, hopefully, set the trend for other companies was provided by the Prudential Insurance Company, which now offers six months of maternity leave and also gives the new mother the option of working at home.

Love me, love my spouse. Many husbands and wives are presenting themselves to prospective employers as package deals. As a result, executive recuitment firms have sprung up to deal with these cases. Now if a company wants a husband to relocate in order to obtain a top executive job, it may need to find an equally rewarding job for his corporate wife. Executive recruiters report that, if the new employer fails to find a suitable post for her, the husband will generally reject the promotion. It seems, at last, that we shouldn't underestimate the power of women and the men who stand with them.

Company day-care centers. When asked what the biggest problem working women face in 1984, noted endricrinologist and feminist Dr. Estelle Ramey answered emphatically: "Child care, child care, child care."

Letty Cottin Pogrebin reports that there are some strides being made in employer-sponsored child care: "Today child-care facilities exist at some twenty corporations, one hundred hospitals, two hundred military installations, and at least one suburban office park complex. . . .

"Given American values, the best motive for establishing corporate child-care centers is the profit motive. The center operated by a Texas medical equipment manufacturer, for example, charges fifteen dollars per week per child, is open 6:30 A.M. to 6:00 P.M. for infants through age six, and is utilized by the children of janitors and executives alike. The center has reduced labor turnover by 23 percent, saved fifteen thousand hours in absenteeism, and helped the company attract the largest pool of qualified applicants it has ever had."

Other options Pogrebin has for companies to make working couples lives better include:

"*Cafeteria-style Benefit Plans.*   Since benefits can account for up to 30 percent of your compensation, why shouldn't you be able to choose only what you and your family need? For instance, if you are covered by your spouse's medical insurance, you might take full insurance instead. If you have young children, you could elect orthodonture coverage and relinquish some retirement money. If you are putting a child through college, you might trade vacation time for cash."

". . . *Parenthood seminars.*   Exxon, Bankers Trust, Texas Commerce Bank, Philip Morris and American Express are among the companies that have begun sponsoring parent education courses, on company time, to help employees learn to balance their family and work more effectively."

An innovative approach offered by Pogrebin suggests a modification to the educational system and the community: "If schools taught housework as *survival skills*, everyone would know how to make a bed . . . ; scour a sink; sweep; use a stove safely, cook basic meals, and clean up after themselves (so they don't become men who wait for some woman to come home and 'feed' them); launder, iron, mend, balance a checkbook, and do basic home maintenance and repairs (so a grown woman doesn't have to sit in the dark waiting for a man to come home and flick on the circuit-breaker switch).

"Why not have family cafeterias built into every housing complex; child care available at an hourly rate . . . ; delivery and repair services that schedule definite appointments . . ."[10]

We can't expect our companies to give us what we need, however. The only way we are ever going to get what we want is to ask for it. Let's face it. Social reform never took place because a government thought it would be nice to give the people what they wanted.

As a case in point, women would never have gotten the vote if they had waited until someone thought it was high time. Had we waited, we would still be churning butter by hand and darning socks at home. Women who think all good things come to those who wait are probably still waiting for Godot or Lefty or the Robert E. Lee.

Dr. Estelle Ramey once told me, "People have to demand what they need, and women have been reluctant to ask for help. What I see as absolutely essential is to push for more and more social awareness of the necessity of providing community services for working families, not just working women."

My personal feeling is that right now, we should ask for what we want and find ways to make our lives more workable. We have the power to create the kinds of lives we want to live. The choice is up to us. At the 1981 Women's Political Caucus in Albuquerque, Eleanor Holmes Norton read one of her poems, which, I think, beautifully summarizes the choices we, as women, have.

A woman is a person who makes choices
A woman is a dreamer
A woman is a planner
A woman is a maker and a molder
A woman is a person who makes choices

A woman heals others
A woman builds bridges
A woman makes children and makes cars
A woman writes poetry and songs
A woman is a person who makes choices.

Is It Really Worth It?

So, in the final analysis, is a dual-career marriage worth it? *Absolutely!* Once you've worked out all the initial snags (which you should have done by virtue of reaching the end of this chapter), it can be great. You and your husband are both presumably working at jobs you enjoy, contributing to the household expenses, and remaining stimulating, productive people. Maybe we can't quite have it all, but a dual-career marriage, with all its flaws, is about as close as we'll ever get in this imperfect world.

Reading more into the situation.   A few books that you might buy for more information on this important subject include:

Family Politics by Letty Cottin Pogrebin, McGraw-Hill, 1983.

Getting Yours by Letty Cottin Pogrebin, Avon Books, 1975.

The Balancing Act: A Handbook for Working Mothers by Niki Scott, Sheed, Andrews & McMeel, 1978.

The Two-Career Couple by Francine and Douglas Hall, A&W, 1979.

The Second Stage by Betty Friedan, Summit Books, 1981.

The Two-Paycheck Marriage by Caroline Bird, Pocket Books, 1980.

"It all comes down to who does the dishes."   *Norman Mailer*

Bibliography

Alberti, Robert E., and Michael Emmons. *Your Perfect Right: A Guide to Assertive Behavior.* San Luis Obispo: Impact Publications, Inc., 1982.

American Telephone and Telegraph. *Views from Women Achievers.* 1977.

Baldrige, Letitia. *The Amy Vanderbilt Complete Book of Etiquette.* New York: Doubleday, 1978.

Bird, Caroline. *The Two-Paycheck Marriage.* New York: Pocket Books, 1980.

Bliss, Edwin C. *Getting Things Done.* New York: Charles Scribner's Sons, 1983.

Bolles, Richard. *What Color Is Your Parachute?* Berkeley, California: Ten Speed Press, 1983.

Burg, Dale. "When the Ax Falls," *Working Woman* (December 1983): 100–104.

Cabot, Tracy. *How to Make a Man Fall in Love With You.* New York: St. Martin's Press, 1984.

Conran, Shirley. *Superwoman.* New York: Crown Publishers, 1978.

Crain, Sharie, with Phillip T. Drotning. *Taking Stock: A Woman's Guide to Corporate Success.* Chicago: Contemporary Books, 1977.

Ettore, Barbara. "Fear of Firing," *Savvy* (September 1983): 85–90.

Farley, Lin. *Sexual Shakedown: The Sexual Harassment of Women on the Job.* New York: Warner Books, 1980.

Foxworth, Jo. *Boss Lady.* New York: Warner Books, 1979.

———. *Wising Up.* New York: Delta, 1981.

Friedan, Betty. *The Second Stage.* New York: Summit Books, 1982.

Halberstam, David. *The Powers That Be.* New York: Alfred A. Knopf, 1979.

Hall, Francine S., and Douglas T. Hall. *The Two-Career Couple.* New York: A&W Publications, 1979.

Handler, Janice, "A Plea for Good Manners," *Savvy* (December 1983): 13.

Harragan, Betty Lehan. *Games Mother Never Taught You: Corporate Gamesmanship for Women.* New York: Warner Books, 1978.

Hennig, Margaret, and Anne Jardim. *The Managerial Woman*. New York: Pocket Books, 1980.

Higginson, Margaret V., and Thomas L. Quick. *The Ambitious Woman's Guide to a Successful Career*. New York: American Management, 1980.

Irish, Richard K. *Go Hire Yourself an Employer*. New York: Doubleday/ Anchor Press, 1978.

———. *If Things Don't Improve Soon, I May Ask You to Fire Me: The Management Book for Everyone Who Works*. New York: Doubleday, 1975.

Korda, Michael. *Male Chauvinism: How It Works*. New York: Random House, 1973.

———. *Power! How to Get It, How to Use It*. New York: Random House, 1975.

Linver, Sandy. *Speak Easy, How to Talk Your Way to the Top*. New York: Summit, 1979.

Nelson, Paula. *The Joy of Money*. New York: Bantam, 1977.

Pogrebin, Letty Cottin. *Getting Yours*. New York: Avon Books, 1975.

———. *Family Politics*. New York: McGraw-Hill, 1983.

Porter, Sylvia. *Sylvia Porter's New Money Book for the 80's*. New York: Avon Books, 1980.

Quinn, Jane Bryant. *Everyone's Money Book*. New York: Delacorte, 1979.

Sarnoff, Dorothy. *Speech Can Change Your Life*. New York: Doubleday, 1970.

"Time Pressured Lives," *Savvy* (December 1980): 28–35.

Schlayer, Mary Elizabeth, with Marilyn H. Cooley. *How to Be a Financially Secure Woman*. New York: Ballantine, 1978.

Schultz, Terri. "In Defense of the Office Romance," *Savvy* (May 1982): 54–64.

Scott, Niki. *The Balancing Act: A Handbook for Working Mothers*. Kansas City: Sheed, Andrews & McMeel, 1978.

Steinem, Gloria. *Outrageous Acts and Everyday Rebellions*. New York: Holt, Rinehart and Winston, 1983.

Stone, Janet, and Jane Bachner. *Speaking Up*. New York: McGraw-Hill, 1977.

Thompson, Melvin R. *Why Should I Hire You?* New York: Jove Publishers, 1975.

Townsend, Robert. *Up the Organization*. New York: Fawcett, 1978.

Trahey, Jane. *Jane Trahey on Women and Power*. New York: Avon Books, 1978.

Walters, Barbara. *How to Talk with Practically Anybody About Practically Anything*. New York: Doubleday, 1983.

Williams, Marcille Gray. *The New Executive Woman*. New York: New American Library, 1978.

Winston, Stephanie. *Getting Organized*. New York: Warner Books, 1980.

——. *The Organized Executive*. New York: Norton, 1983.

Yankelovich, Daniel. *New Rules: Searching for Self-fulfillment in a World Turned Upside Down*. New York: Random House, 1981.

Notes

Chapter 1. Fire Drill

1. Richard K. Irish, *Go Hire Yourself an Employer*, 65, 124.
2. Jo Foxworth, *Boss Lady*, 66.
3. Foxworth, 77.
4. Jo Foxworth, *Wising Up*, 168.
5. Irish, *Go Hire Yourself an Employer*.
6. Richard K. Irish, *If Things Don't Improve Soon I May Ask You to Fire Me*, 2.
7. Robert Townsend, *Up The Organization*, 63.
8. Irish, *If Things Don't Improve*, 2, 3, 7.
9. Dale Burg, "When The Ax Falls," *Working Woman* (December 1983): 100.
10. Betty Lehan Harragan, *Games Mother Never Taught You*, 204.
11. Jane Trahey, *Women and Power*, 160, 161.
12. Ibid., 155.

Chapter 2. Checks and Balances

1. Trahey, *Women and Power*, 20.
2. Paula Nelson, *The Joy of Money*, 4.
3. Foxworth, *Wising Up*, 7, 8.
4. Sharie Crain, *Taking Stock*, 141.
5. Nelson, *The Joy of Money*, 98, 99.
6. Crain, *Taking Stock*, 136, 137.
7. Irish, *Go Hire Yourself An Employer*, 94.
8. Mary Elizabeth Schlayer and Marilyn H. Cooley, *How To Be A Financially Secure Woman*, 94, 95.
9. Nelson, *The Joy of Money*, 30–32.

Chapter 3. Judging a Book by Its Cover

1. Janet Stone and Jane Bachner, *Speaking Up*, 122.
2. Ibid.

3. Letitia Baldrige, *The Amy Vanderbilt Complete Book of Etiquette*, 483, 484.
4. Marcille Gray Williams, *The New Executive Woman*, 147.
5. Foxworth, *Boss Lady*, 88.
6. Crain, *Taking Stock*, 109.
7. Margaret Hennig and Anne Jardim, *The Managerial Woman*, 52.
8. Williams, *The New Executive Woman*, 74.
9. Robert E. Alberti and Michael Emmons, *Your Perfect Right*.
10. Foxworth, *Wising Up*, 115.
11. Crain, *Taking Stock*, 91–93.
12. Sandy Linver, *Speak Easy*, 19.
13. Dorothy Sarnoff, *Speech Can Change Your Life*, 6.
14. Stone and Bachner, *Speaking Up*, 11, 12.
15. Harragan, *Games Mother Never Taught You*, 300.
16. Gloria Steinem, *Outrageous Acts and Everyday Rebellions*, 9–11.
17. Barbara Walters, *How to Talk to Practically Anyone About Practically Anything*, 107.
18. Stone and Bachner, *Speaking Up*, 136.
19. Ibid.

Chapter 4. Power Failure

1. Steinem, *Outrageous Acts*, 149.
2. Trahey, *Women and Power*, 17, 18.
3. Michael Korda, *Power*, 255, 256.
4. Harragan, *Games Mother Never Taught You*, 35.
5. Foxworth, *Wising Up*, 155.
6. Trahey, *Women and Power*, 14.
7. Steinem, *Outrageous Acts*, 116.
8. Harragan, *Games Mother Never Taught You*.

Chapter 5. Sex Fifth Avenue

1. Letty Cottin Pogrebin, *Getting Yours*, 92.
2. Trahey, *Women and Power*, 72.
3. Lin Farley, *Sexual Shakedown*, 115.
4. *Ibid.*, 117.
5. *Views From Women Achievers*, 104.
6. Farley, *Sexual Shakedown*, 118.
7. Margaret V. Higginson and Thomas L. Quick, *The Ambitious Women's Guide to a Successful Career*, 148.
8. Foxworth, *Boss Lady*, 161.
9. Hennig and Jardim, *The Managerial Woman*, 202.

10. Michael Korda, *Male Chauvinism*, 111.
11. Pogrebin, *Getting Yours*, 94, 95.
12. Harragan, *Games Mother Never Taught You*.
13. *Views from Women Achievers*, 105.
14. Baldrige, *The Amy Vanderbilt Complete Book of Etiquette*, 451.
15. Ibid.

Chapter 6. Time Waits for No Woman

1. Stephanie Winston, *The Organized Executive*, 36, 40–42.
2. Edwin C. Bliss, *Getting Things Done*, 184, 185.
3. Ibid., 58, 59.
4. Townsend, *Up the Organization*, 130.
5. Foxworth, *Boss Lady*, 129.
6. Townsend, *Up the Organization*, 154.
7. Shirley Conran, *Superwoman*, 235, 236.

Chapter 7. You Work. He Works.

1. Conran, *Superwoman*, 235.
2. Letty Cottin Pogrebin, *Family Politics*, 148.
3. Ibid., 129.
4. *Views From Women Achievers*, 18, 19.
5. Conran, *Superwoman*, 235, 236.
6. John Sherman, "Got The Babysitting Blues?" *Albuquerque Journal*, April 10, 1984.
7. Pogrebin, *Family Politics*, 129.
8. Betty Friedan, *The Second Stage*.
9. Daniel Yankelovich, *New Rules*, 94.
10. Pogrebin, *Family Politics*, 138, 140, 141, 172, 173.

Index

About the Author

PEGGY VAN HULSTEYN is a seminar conductor and business consultant who travels around the country giving lectures and workshops helping working women organize their lives. She also writes feature and travel articles for major monthly magazines and major dailies. She has been assistant travel editor at *Mademoiselle;* Southeastern director of publicity for American International Pictures; copywriter for Tucker Wayne Advertising Agency in Atlanta; and owner of an award-winning advertising agency in Austin.